# *Introduction to*
# Environmental Design

**DON C. FAULKNER, AIA**
**Associate Professor**

*Department of Architecture and Landscape Architecture*
*North Dakota State University*

KENDALL/HUNT PUBLISHING COMPANY
4050 Westmark Drive Dubuque, Iowa 52002

# Contents

# PART 1

# Defining Environmental Design

The beginning sections of most introductory courses involve defining the various terms that are used in the field being studied. We will start there as well but first it is important to set the stage for understanding the terms and ideas of Environmental Design. Environmental Design is comprised of several fields of study and work. Each of these fields vie with each other for their slice of the work and their preeminence. Even in the midst of this fierce competition, practitioners of environmental design share some very significant goals, desires and commitments that seem to pull the various design fields together as a cohesive field that we call Environmental Design. Most successful environmental designers are passionate about design quality within their individual field and expect high quality design work from all of their allied professionals as well. Environmental designers today also share a deep concern for the fragile nature of our environment, the planet that we live on, its systems and its cultures. They share concern and also share responsibility for the improvement or degradation of a significant portion of our future. This is an awesome responsibility. It is also the context within which we begin our description of what Environmental Design is and what Environmental Designers do.

To gain a level of understanding of any subject we have to develop a working knowledge of the language used in that subject. Environmental design is like most fields of endeavor, it has its own vocabulary, its own phrases, and its own shorthand. Unlike other fields, environmental design also requires the understanding of a visual language; one not unlike a foreign language. In Part 1 of this book we will start to define the terms of environmental design, the written and spoken language of the field. Later, in Part 4, we will deal more specifically with the visual language of the field.

A shortcoming of many specialized fields of endeavor is that they become too mired in their own language. They become so insular that the majority of the population cannot understand the conversations of the field. We have all had experiences when we wander into conversations between doctors who are talking about the new drug hexahubiwhatsadoey and its effects on the adrenal system. Or we happen on a conversation with accountants discussing actuarial tables and the latest rulings of accounting's governing body and our eyes glaze over and our mind wanders. The environmental design fields are just as guilty of this as any other field. Although it is probably not fair to quote out of context or to single out this particular passage when so many are worse, the following passage was contained in a book that I just finished reading about a design competition. ". . . a free-build zone allowing a variety of interests to integrate themselves in proximity to the host. Whether by "franchise-pods,' a 'liquid wrap,' 'index environments' or experimental terrain for new media and technologies (and their concomitant commercial objectives) the renovated space would serve as a condenser for 'imaginative collaborative, civic and individual, social and economic [systems] integrating with subcultures.'"[1] What in the world is being said here? Since it is important for everyone to be involved with their own environment it is also important to be able to talk about it in a way that is understandable. This book will try to introduce the language of design in terms that can be understood by anyone. We will also try not to get bogged down in our own techno-speak, or "archi-babble" which was the way that Peter Blake described writing styles in architectural publications.[2]

[1]Techentin, Warren ed. (2004). *Dead Malls.* Los Angeles: Los Angeles Forum for Architecture and Urban Design. Page 30.
[2]Blake, Peter. (1990). Comment made during a lecture at North Dakota State University, Fargo, North Dakota.

# Chapter 1

# Environmental Design and Its Fields

The task of defining the term "environmental design" is not a particularly easy one. Some people within the environmental design fields might think it foolish to even try to define such an ambiguous thing. The term "environmental design" is actually a fairly recent invention. Prior to the 1970's a single term that described the various professions that impact the building of our world did not exist. It was the ecology movement that coined the term environmental design. The realization, by early ecologists, that the natural systems of our world were inextricably linked with one another pointed to a need to see our design efforts in a broader context. We suddenly saw our efforts to build better buildings, cities, landscapes and products as related endeavors linked to our overall environment. Like most terms that relate to large ideas and generalist concepts, "environmental design" does not have a universally agreed upon definition. You will find different definitions given by people that are involved with environmental engineering, or environmental conservation, or environmental science, etc. The definition that follows is one that might make sense to a planner, an urban designer, a landscape architect, an architect, an interior designer or a product designer.

Figure 1.1 . . .

A fictional view exploring the fields of environmental design. Viewed from an interior space, we look out the window at the work of a planner, a landscape architect, an architect and an urban designer.

# DEFINITIONS

ENVIRONMENTAL DESIGN is a broadly defined field of work consisting of professional designers that are engaged in determining the future of our physical environment. Environmental design is the umbrella field that includes many different design professions including: planning, landscape architecture, urban design, architecture, civil engineering, and interior design.

*Figure 1.2 . . .*

An environment designed by planners and urban designers. Salt Lake City.

*Figure 1.3 . . .*

An environment largely designed by civil engineers. Duluth.

*Figure 1.4 . . .*

An environment designed by architects. Salt Lake City.

*Figure 1.5 . . .*

An environment designed by landscape architects. Paris.

*Figure 1.6 . . .*

An environment designed by interior designers. San Francisco.

*Figure 1.7 . . .*

An environment designed by urban designers and architects. Chicago.

This is not an exhaustive list of environmental design professions, the field can include many others. There are times when we may want to include transportation planners, mechanical engineers, electrical engineers, product designers, environmental signage designers, and infrastructure planners in our discussions of environmental design. However, for this introduction to environmental design we will focus our discussions on planning, landscape architecture, urban design, architecture and interior design as the primary fields of environmental design with some coverage of engineering. Anyone whose design work impacts the physical environment around us is an environmental designer. These environmental designers have a legal responsibility to protect the health, safety and welfare of society. The legal responsibility manifests itself in the licensure of most of the environmental design professionals. There are national licensing tests in architecture, landscape architecture and interior design but licenses to practice in each of these fields is granted by individual states using, in part, the national tests. Planners are not licensed but there is a national test of competence administered by their professional organization. Environmental designers do indeed have a legal responsibility to society but our moral responsibility to both society and the natural environment in which we live is the foundation of our work. Protecting the health, safety and welfare of society is a daunting task but to do so with no regard for the long-term health of our environment will eventually result in a failure to protect health, safety and welfare. Our moral imperative to be good stewards of the land, protectors of natural systems and supporters of diverse cultures far outweighs the legal responsibilities placed on us.

It is useful for us to look a little more closely at both of the terms, design and environment, to help strengthen our understanding of the definition of environmental design.

Let's start by looking at the word "design." Design has many definitions in the dictionary some of which are included here:

> *to create, fashion, execute, or construct according to plan: to devise for a specific function or end: deliberate purposive planning: a preliminary sketch or outline showing the main features of something to be executed: the creative art of executing aesthetic or functional designs.*[3]

There are some very important concepts contained in the dictionary definition for design. Design is a creative act that relates to a function. Design is purposeful and sets the path for future action. Design is also related to aesthetics. For our purposes DESIGN, as it applies to environmental design, is:

> *the purposeful, creative act that predicts and establishes future, useful aesthetic products and physical places.*

The products and places we are talking about are those that we use in our everyday lives. These products and places might include buildings, bridges, parks, cities, telephones, lawnmowers, books, signs, freeways, regions, metropolises, a house, etc. The list of products and places designed by environmental designers is enormous. Environmental designers have an incredible impact on our surroundings. In this book we will be focusing more directly on the places that are designed rather than on the products. The design of environmental products is a subject that requires a book all its own.

Design is indeed a creative act. Designers search for new, functional, efficient, aesthetic solutions to the problems that confront us. Design exists at the crossroads between art and science. It has aspects of both art and science but cannot be said to exist in either field. Artists produce paintings, sculpture, even environments that deal specifically with aesthetics and emotion. Designer's deal with aesthetics and emotion but their work must also serve a functional need within our environment. The function may not always be in service to human beings and is often in service to the natural systems of our world and the maintenance of life on this planet. Scientists deal with the facts and fabric of the systems that we utilize every day. They are ultimately interested in understanding how things work and behave in our world. Designers must be firmly grounded in scientific principle to ensure that our functional products actually work, stand up and remain viable for hundreds of years. Designers place equal importance on the function and aesthetics of our work.

---

[3]Mish, Frederick, ed. (1993). *Merriam-Webster's Collegiate Dictionary, Tenth Edition*. Springfield, MA: Merriam-Webster, Incorporated. Page 313.

Designers work in the present to solve a problem some time in the future. It was once explained to me that designers must peer into the crystal ball to find out what is needed in the future if they are to be successful in the present. Designers seldom produce the things that they design. Architects design a building and prepare all of the plans and specifications necessary for someone else (a series of contractors) to build the building sometime in the future. The same is true for planners, landscape architects, engineers, and interior designers. The time from inception of the design of a building until it is completed may take two to five years. The time from inception to completion of a landscape design might take many years to allow the trees and shrubs to grow and mature. The landscape architect must envision the design with small immature plants as well as with mature plants. The subject of time within environmental design will be dealt with more fully in a later chapter.

We will now move to the word "environment." The dictionary definitions of environment include:

> *the circumstances, objects, or conditions by which one is surrounded: the complex of physical, chemical, and biotic factors that act upon an organism or an ecological community and ultimately determine its form and survival: the aggregate of social and cultural conditions that influence the life of an individual or community.*[4]

The ENVIRONMENT that we are talking about in "environmental design" is:

> *the world around us, the places where we live, work, play, love, hate, build and destroy.*

I include a series of contradictory terms here because environmental designers have the power to impact our physical environment in extremely positive ways or in ways that destroy it. Often in our attempt to build good physical environments for human beings we damage the natural environment in ways that are possibly detrimental to our future existence. It is only in the past two decades that environmental designers have begun to understand the impact that we can have, both positively and negatively on our physical environment.

The environment that environmental designers deal with certainly includes the specific place that our projects inhabit. It also includes the area surrounding the project and places thousands of miles away that are impacted by our design decisions. This environment includes animals (including people), plants and geology and the systems that relate one to another.

Traditionally, environmental design is not a single field. It is a collection of fields each individually defined and developed with overlapping areas of concern. It is important that we start to understand environmental design as a single field with various professionals focusing on specific parts of the field.

## THE ENVIRONMENTAL DESIGN PROFESSIONS

Environmental design, it could be argued, started with city planning during the Roman Empire. The imposition of a grid structure on the Roman Castra is one of the first examples of humans predetermining their physical environment. Other examples of environmental design during the Roman Empire are the building of aqueducts to bring clean water from distant sources into Roman cities. Roman aqueducts and roads could be claimed to be the

[4]Ibid. Page 388.

first civil engineering projects. It might also be argued that the master builders of the Greek Empire, with their highly developed classical orders of architecture, were the first environmental designers. I suppose we could even say that the first interior designer determined where the fire was to be located in the cave. It isn't very important to determine exactly who was the first environmental designer. It is important to know that humans have been engaged in planning their physical environment for a long, long time.

Over the years various designers have concentrated on parts of the physical environment, developing separate and distinct design fields. Planning, civil engineering and architecture find their roots in the more distant past. In more recent times the environmental design fields of landscape architecture, interior design, urban design and environmental graphics have been established. The boundary between each of the environmental design fields is not well defined and quite frankly cannot be specifically defined. The nature of environmental design work keeps it from being easily compartmentalized. City planners are concerned with the physical form of the city; with its layout and functioning. The form of the city impacts the quality of the spaces created within the city, which is the concern of the urban designer and the landscape architect. The spaces within the city impact the ability of the architect to create functional and aesthetic buildings, which, in turn, impacts the work of the interior designer. Getting around in the buildings and the city is augmented by environmental graphics. Any time you walk down a city street you are encountering the work of literally hundreds of environmental designers. Each designer's work has had impact on everyone else's work.

# THE ATTRACTION OF ENVIRONMENTAL DESIGN

Who are these people that become environmental designers? Many areas of study and work require very specific talents and abilities from the people that choose to work in the field. A good example of this would be a research scientist in a field such as chemistry or physics. Research scientists must bring a very logical mind and a set of personal habits that allow the person to be highly meticulous in their work. They also rely on mathematics and a tremendous body of specific knowledge within their field. Another example might be a painter. Artists, such as a painter, rely on their creative urges and a willingness to explore things that other people will not or do not see. Artists also need to be excellent crafts people, having trained their mind, their eye and their hand in connection with the tools of their field.

One of the most compelling aspects of environmental design for many people is that it is a cross between science and art. Environmental designers must be creative craftspeople much like artists and yet must be logical and scientific when building within the physical environment. The ability to see potential solutions to problems anywhere and at any time is an advantage for an environmental designer. This unification of science and art along with the many varied fields of environmental design allows the field to be an exciting alternative for many different people. The more scientifically inclined individuals tend to be drawn to the more technical aspects of the field while the more artistically inclined tend to be drawn to the creative problem solving.

Social scientists have postulated that there are four different types of thinkers. The SOCIAL THINKERS, people that first think in terms of the people that will be affected by an action. Social thinkers often involve other people in their thinking process. CONCEPTUAL THINKERS are people that first think of the global implications of an action. Conceptual thinkers see the larger framework of a problem and are not afraid to make mistakes in exploring solutions. STRUCTURAL THINKERS are people that think in a very organized and ordered way. Structural thinkers like flow charts and careful organization. And finally, the ANALYTICAL THINKERS are the people that rely on the facts of the situation and logic to make decisions. Analytical thinkers not only want all of the facts and figures related to a problem but they want to know why we should solve the problem.[5] Over the past several years we have conducted tests in our environmental design studios at North Dakota State University and have found that we always have people from each of the four groups of thinkers in the studio. Environmental design encourages people from all cultures, backgrounds and thought processes to become involved in the field. In order to solve the extremely complex problems of environmental design it is important to have people with a variety of skills and abilities involved together in the solutions.

## A BROADER VIEW OF ENVIRONMENTAL DESIGN

This short discussion of the founding of environmental design points out a current problem encountered within the field. Each segment of environmental design is a separate field, each with overlapping areas of interest and expertise. This condition leads to enmity between the various environmental design fields with litigation between professional societies being all too common. We have discovered that the best design solutions for our society and our world require the participation of many different environmental designers and consultants. Environmental designers need to work together in team situations to solve very complex and important problems related to our physical environment.

This need to work together to solve problems is the primary reason that this book advocates a new definition for environmental design. The hope is that we will be better able to work together and to minimize arguments about areas of expertise if we all see ourselves as environmental designers first and specialists second. This may have some impact on the way we license environmental designers. It will also have some impact on how we educate environmental designers. It seems essential that we pursue this change with a great deal of vigor and commitment. The writing of this book is an attempt to begin this process of change.

To understand how one environmental designer's work impacts other environmental designers, as noted above, is very important. It is equally important to understand that decisions made by environmental designers can potentially impact people and environmental systems throughout the globe.

[5]Research work conducted by Geil Browning as presented in James, Jennifer (1996). *Thinking in the Future Tense*. Touchstone/Simon and Schuster, New York.

# Man's Impact on the Environment

To explore just how inter-related our actions are as environmental designers, let's look at a few scenarios in which we may be involved. A planner might decide to encourage growth in an outlying section of a city. If the planners have included mass transit, schools, and commercial areas to serve this new section of the city then they have made decisions that can reduce our reliance on the automobile. That, in turn, reduces the consumption of gasoline, a non-renewable resource, and reduces the amount of air pollution. A decision to reduce our reliance on the car can have significant impact on the worldwide availability of oil products. It also reduces air pollution, which is spread throughout the world by the jet stream winds. The civil engineer can design transportation systems that encourage pedestrian traffic and eliminate the need to drive an automobile everywhere. Walking promotes social connection and physical well being and also leads to decreased pollution from the car. The landscape architect, in designing the parks for this new section of town and in setting the standards for planting in the area, can minimize the impact of flooding, reduce our reliance on fertilizer, impact the temperature of the entire area and provide oxygen through re-forestation. Fertilizers and other water-borne pollutants find their way into the water system of the globe. A reduction in fertilizer and careful control of run-off can benefit all of the world. Significant plant life in an area can also mediate temperatures which in turn reduces both heating costs in the winter and cooling costs in the summer—again reducing the consumption of non-renewable resources and the production of pollutants. The architect, through careful design of the buildings can reduce our consumption of non-renewable resources as well as assure the recyclability of the materials that are used in construction. The architect can also have tremendous impact on the amount of energy that is used in the production of the buildings as well as in their maintenance. The interior designer can have similar impact by carefully choosing the materials to be used inside the buildings. Assuring the use of recyclable and renewable resources and not using endangered materials such as Brazilian rosewood or even redwood. You can easily see that using redwood in decks, for example, on millions of homes throughout the world would quickly deplete the remaining giant redwood trees. It takes hundreds of years to grow a redwood tree, a natural condition that limits the availability of the wood for human use. This is a fairly simple illustration of the ways that the decisions of each environmental designer impact the decisions of other designers and impact the environmental systems of the world.

Environmental design problems have been called "wicked problems" by researchers in artificial intelligence because the problems involve so many variables and no discreet, correct answer. Environmental design requires people to have a very broad knowledge base with a great deal of specialized knowledge as well. The fracturing of environmental design into specialties helps to deal with the immense amount of specialized knowledge required in each design field. The existence of specialties does not however deal with the need for broad-based knowledge and the ability to see problems more holistically. The pulling together of the specialties into the larger field of environmental design allows us to think more globally. It allows us all to recognize the tremendous contributions of other designers to our own work. It allows all environmental designers to do a better job.

# THE GAIA THEORY

Gaia (pronounced jee'-uh) is the Greek goddess known as Mother Earth. She was born from the chaos of the empty universe along with Eros. It seems important to me that the earth and love were the foundation for the universe to the Greeks. As the mother of earth, Gaia gave birth to the sea, the sky, and the mountains. She was worshiped throughout Greece as the mother of the earth and for being the source of all of the Greek Gods. Over time her importance waned. Maybe this was a result of a change in the attitudes developed in our culture. Western culture, in particular, began to believe that our relationship to the earth was one of challenge and control not one of integration. In Roman mythology Gaia became known as Tellus or Terra, another term we associate with the earth today.[6] Tellus/Terra never had the importance of Gaia and our attitudes toward the earth have continued to disconnect us from mother nature ever since.

The Greek mythology centered on Gaia is important to us now as both a way of looking at the earth and as a scientific theory developed by James Lovelock linking all forms of life together in one system. "We have since defined Gaia as a complex entity involving the Earth's biosphere, atmosphere, oceans, and soil; the totality constituting a feedback or cybernetic system which seeks an optimal physical and chemical environment for life on this planet. The maintenance of relatively constant conditions by active control may be conveniently described by the term 'homoeostasis'."[7] Gaia is a self-regulating system that includes all life, the rocks, the oceans, and the air, all of the surface of the earth in a kind of super organism that seeks to keep the system stable enough to support life. Although many, if not most, scientists accept the Gaia Theory there is still concern about linking the scientific theory with an ancient Greek Goddess, so much of the research is conducted under the banners of Earth System Science or Geophysiology.

The scientific research has shown us a remarkable system that adjusts itself to maintain the optimum conditions for the support of life. The balance of chemicals in the air, the nutrients in the soil, and the variation in temperature to name only three of thousands of critical relationships stay within a narrow band of variation that allows life to continue on this planet. Professor Lovelock, in the preface to the 1995 edition of his book, observes ". . . twenty-six years ago, the future looked good. There were problems looming with people and the environment but all seemed capable of sensible or scientific solution. Now the prospect is, at best, doubtful. One of the few certainties about the Earth is that we have changed the atmosphere and the land surface more than it has changed by itself in million of years. These changes still go on and ever faster as our numbers grow."[8] Scientists estimate that the earth can only compensate for one-third of the carbon that we are currently pumping into the atmosphere. We have moved beyond a point where Gaia can self correct for the damage that we have caused. Pollution caused by industry and by automobiles is responsible for at least half of the greenhouse gases being pumped into the atmosphere. In comparison, buildings are responsible for at least one-third of all energy consumed in the world. That energy consumption contributes substantially to the greenhouse emissions. Environmental designers have direct control over decisions about buildings, interiors and landscapes. They also have the ability to reduce automobile usage through sound planning and urban design decisions. The licensing laws of environmental

[6]Leadbetter, Ron. *Gaia*. (1997). An online article in Encyclopedia Mythica at http://www.pantheon.org/articles/g/gaia.html accessed 18 February 2007.

[7]Lovelock, James. (1979/1995). *Gaia: A New Look At Life On Earth*. Oxford University Press, Oxford, England. Page 10.

[8]Ibid. Page xviii.

*Figure 1.8 . . .*

The sea.

*Figure 1.9 . . .*

The sky.

*Figure 1.10 . . .*

The mountains.

designers require them to protect the health, safety and welfare of the public. If environmental designers contribute to the endangerment of the planet they are not doing their job. It makes sense that we must include sustaining the earth as a part of our professional responsibility.

## SOCIAL RESPONSIBILITY AND ECO-LITERACY

Environmental designers have always answered to two masters: the clients that we serve and the society at large. These two masters often are in competition with each other and it is our job to mediate between them. I think one problem that the environmental design fields have had is that the practitioners have sided with the clients a bit too much in the past. In fact, they have sided with the client way too much. We are discovering that we have not been living up to our ethical and moral standards to protect our society and our earth. It is easy to say that we didn't know that what we were doing was harmful, and in many cases we really did not know that it was harmful. But, ignorance is not an excuse. We have more and more knowledge and a greater understanding now of the consequences of our actions than we ever have had in the past. If we continue to make decisions biased to one of our masters then we truly are failing as designers. Kevin Flynn, the first LEED (Leadership in Energy and Environmental Design) certified architect in Minnesota, bases his practice around creating the best economic reasons for his clients to be sustainable. He has been able to make substantial progress in sustainable architecture by showing his clients that sound sustainable decisions can save them money in the very near future for little or no expenditure today. Kevin is showing his clients that our commitment to sustainability is not only essential to our survival, but that it makes good business sense as well.

Social responsibility is somewhat different for each of the environmental design fields. Planners, landscape architects and urban designers work primarily for the public, but to know what is best for everyone is a formidable challenge. It is a challenge that carries with it a presumption of being correct and that is just not the case for many individuals. It is particularly hard to have large groups of people accept changes in their environment even if those changes are based on solid research, science, economics and a respect for the future. Architects and interior designers work for smaller groups of people and it may be a little bit easier to reason with your clients to approach their future in a different way—but it is still a big challenge. These challenges, related to our social responsibility, require environmental designers to become educators of all the people that we work with. We must become immersed in the connectedness of our world. We must be a part of Gaia and we must show others how our decisions impact not only them but the world around us.

There is a new term being used to describe a body of knowledge that is necessary for all of us to possess in order for us to become a sustainable society. That term is eco-literacy. Eco-literacy involves an understanding of our place in the world and a desire to not just do a better job with our environmental design decisions, but to change the very nature of our relationship with Gaia. The relationship that we have with the earth has been rooted in human arrogance. We have traditionally treated the earth as ours to use. Its resources are available to make human life better. Until 1973 the United States government did not acknowledge the right of anything other than humans to exist. In 1973 the Endangered Species Act was passed which helps to protect animal species that are threatened with extinction. Of course it would be nice to protect their existence before they are near extinction. To be truly eco-literate the basic attitudes about our place in the world needs to evolve into a more respectful, dependent and humble point of view. Humanity's point of view can only change with understanding and knowledge. To make good decisions we must have great information. There is too much information involved for us all to become eco-literate by reading this book. In fact, we can only begin to introduce the subject here and hopefully spark some personal interest in learning more.

The ecology movement began in the early 1970's when books like Paul Ehrlich's *The Population Bomb* or *The Limits to Growth* by Donella H. Meadows, Dennis L. Meadows, Jorgen Randers, and William W. Behrens III began to point out serious problems with over-population, pollution, and the consumption of non-renewable resources. Some environmental designers responded by building a few homes with solar heating panels or maybe an occasional wind turbine. It was really unfortunate, but the technology was not ready and the solar heated homes were pretty ugly and didn't work very well. The designers interested in these early environmentally responsive ideas were classified as fringe designers and lumped into a group with hippies and war protestors (the Viet Nam Conflict). As society moved into the rah rah 80's interest in the environment seemed to disappear. We became more and more affluent. We drove bigger cars and more of them. Our cities grew and grew and they sprawled out into open countryside. In the early 1990's we began to hear warnings again about our environment. We were warned of impending global warming and told that the release of "greenhouse gases" into the atmosphere was the culprit.

There was enough concern by 1994 that world leaders convened at The United Nations Convention on Climate Change. The outcome was a framework for governments to work together to deal with the challenges of climate change and specifically the emissions of carbon dioxide and other greenhouse gases into the atmosphere. The framework called for a mandatory reduction of carbon dioxide emissions by those countries that ratified the agreement. Since the conference 189 countries have ratified the United Nations Framework Convention on Climate Change (UNFCCC). This includes most of the major countries of the world with the exception of the United States and Australia. In 1997 the UNFCCC met in Kyoto, Japan to create stricter restrictions on greenhouse gas emissions. The Kyoto Protocol, as it has become known, sets a reduction of 5% in greenhouse gas emissions based on 1990 levels by 2012. The Kyoto Protocol was ratified in February of 2005. The United States and Australia have still not signed the agreements.

While world leaders spent the last 13 years agreeing to reduce greenhouse gases by a paltry 5% we have learned the following facts.[9]

- Carbon dioxide ($CO_2$) is the primary greenhouse gas being emitted into our atmosphere.

- For over 650,000 years the average amount of $CO_2$ in our atmosphere has been 300 parts per million.

- Today the concentration of $CO_2$ in the atmosphere is 370 ppm.

- The United States is responsible for 30% of the world's greenhouse gas emissions.

- Carbon emissions in 2005 were 70 million tons per day. 25 million tons of that go into the oceans and increase the acidity of the ocean.

- Carbon emissions from fossil fuel combustion per person in the United States is 5.6 tons per year.

- Carbon emissions from fossil fuel combustion per person in the world is 1 ton per year.

- Increases in greenhouse gases, particularly carbon dioxide, cause global warming.

- In 2007 the world's scientists and political leaders acknowledged that man is the cause of global warming.

- The average temperature, worldwide, has increased .6° Fahrenheit since 1950.

- The average ocean temperature has increased .3° F from 1990 to 2004.

- The eleven hottest years on record have occurred in the last 15 years. 2006 was the hottest year on record, 2005 was the second hottest year on record.

- The Arctic icecap has decreased by 1.5 million square kilometers since 1970 and approximately half a million square kilometers since 1990.

- The amount of ice melt in Greenland has tripled in the last 14 years.

- The numbers of severe storms and floods in the United States has increased by 43 events per year from the 1980's to the 1990's. Europe saw a similar increase. There were over 120 floods in the U.S. in 2005.

- If the Greenland icecap were to melt completely, sea level would be increased by approximately 20 feet worldwide. Up to 100 million people will be displaced by such a catastrophe.

- The population of the world in 1945 was 2.3 billion people. The population of the world in 2005 was 6.4 billion people. The projected population in 2050 is 9.1 billion people.

- The world's population is expected to stabilize at about 9.1 billion people as a result of the demographic transformation that is occurring now. We are moving from a demographic model of high birthrate and high death rate to a low birthrate and low death rate model worldwide.

[9]Bender, Lawrence and Laurie David, producers. (2006). *An Inconvenient Truth: A Global Warning*. Paramount Classics and Participant Productions, Hollywood, California. DVD.

Since environmental designers create the form of our cities, establish our transportation patterns, decide how and where the landscape is developed, provide shelter and accommodation for people, choose which materials are going to be used in construction, and control how at least one-third of the world's energy is used we are responsible. We are responsible for some of the problem and we are responsible for a large part of the solution. Solving tough problems is our stock in trade. This is one of the toughest we have ever faced. To be successful in this endeavor we will have to set very stringent goals. Given the list of issues related to carbon dioxide one such goal would be to totally eliminate carbon emissions from all buildings and from the processes that support buildings. The next chapter lists several goals that could be undertaken by environmental designers to help ensure that our children's children have a planet on which to live. The changes in our environment caused by global warming are inevitable unless we halt and reverse the causes of global warming.

## SUSTAINABILITY

Sustainability has become the latest in a long line of catch phrases about environmental responsibility. The unfortunate part of the adoption of a term into the public dialogue is that the meaning of the word gets diluted. Sustainability in its current usage means the application of a series of fixes to the design of buildings or environments. Sustainability is much more than that. It involves an altered state of living in the world. It requires different assumptions about what is important to us individually and collectively. William McDonough, in his publication *The Hannover Principles*, defines sustainability in the following way.

> *The concept of sustainability has been introduced to combine concern for the well-being of the planet with continued growth and human development. Though there is much debate as to what the word actually suggests, we can put forth the definition offered by the World Commission on Environment and Development: "Meeting the needs of the present without compromising the ability of future generations to meet their own needs."*

Environmental designers are a very key group in the move toward sustainability. While **design** involves the creation and realization of human needs, **sustainable design** involves the creation and realization of environmentally responsible human needs as an integral part of Mother Earth. Not only is the integration of human need and desire important in sustainable design, but it also includes *growth* and *development* of humankind. Sustainability does not mean a return to a simpler time. It means creation in a responsible, interconnected way.

To be truly sustainable environmental designers we have to become truly eco-literate. As that happens our lifestyles will change. We will not think in the same ways that we do now. This is already happening but probably not quickly enough. I have heard several prominent environmental designers say that doing "less bad" is not the same thing as doing "good." I like to equate this to the first time that I was in London leading a group of students on a foreign study tour. We arrived in London, went down to the "Tube" (London's subway system) and got on the train going the wrong way. It would not have done us any good to have the train slow down, we would still be going in the wrong direction. It would not have done us any good to have some of us get off the train and get on one going the right direction. It would have done us "good" to all get off of the train, learn where we all needed to go to get on the correct train. And, that is just what we did. We don't need to slow down the direction that we are headed with the environment and global warming, we need to turn the direction around. One way to turn the train around is for all environmental designers to share a new definition of the goals, foundations and principles underlying our daily work. Just such a definition was developed by William McDonough.

# HANNOVER PRINCIPLES

In 1991, William McDonough was commissioned to write a set of principles to guide the development of the facilities for a World's Fair in Hannover, Germany. Hannover was chosen as the site of the world exposition for the year 2000. Since the fair was set for the beginning of a new millennium, the city chose "Humanity, Nature, and Technology" as the theme for the exposition. By making the decision to focus on one of the great challenges of the future rather than on the accomplishments of the past, the city of Hannover took a giant step toward their own future of sustainability in the new millennium. The guidelines that were developed sought to create a focus for all aspects of the exposition. They provide an underlying foundation for design and planning decisions for the exposition and for Hannover. The document that was produced has become known as the *Hannover Principles* and has gained strength and importance as a manifesto of sustainable design thought for the world. William McDonough is first of all a designer. He is an architect that has expanded his work into the design of systems, buildings, products and communities. The Hannover Principles:

1.  **Insist on the rights of humanity and nature to coexist** in a healthy, supportive, diverse and sustainable condition.

2.  **Recognize interdependence.** The elements of human design interact with and depend upon the natural world, with broad and diverse implications at every scale. Expand design considerations to recognizing even distant effects.

3.  **Respect the relationship between spirit and matter.** Consider all aspects of human settlement including community, dwelling, industry and trade in terms of existing and evolving connections between spiritual and material consciousness.

4.  **Accept responsibility for the consequences of design** decisions upon human well-being, the viability of natural systems and their right to co-exist.

5.  **Create safe objects of long-term value.** Do not burden future generations with requirements for maintenance or vigilant administration of potential danger due to the careless creation of products, processes or standards.

6.  **Eliminate the concept of waste.** Evaluate and optimize the full life-cycle of products and processes, to approach the state of natural systems, in which there is no waste.

7.  **Rely on natural energy flows.** Human designs should, like the living world, derive their creative forces from perpetual solar income. Incorporate this energy efficiently and safely for responsible use.

8.  **Understand the limitations of design.** No human creation lasts forever and design does not solve all problems. Those who create and plan should practice humility in the face of nature. Treat nature as a model and mentor, not as an inconvenience to be evaded or controlled.

9.  **Seek constant improvement by the sharing of knowledge.** Encourage direct and open communication between colleagues, patrons, manufacturers and users to link long term sustainable considerations with ethical responsibility, and re-establish the integral relationship between natural processes and human activity.[10]

---

[10]McDonough, William. (1992). *The Hannover Principles: Design for Sustainability*. William McDonough & Partners, Charlottesville, Virginia.

Mr. McDonough approaches all of his work as a designer. He is looking for solutions to problems that are cost effective, perform well and are aesthetically pleasing. This is a common set of goals for any designer. Mr. McDonough, however, adds three more criteria in order to create successful design solutions. Is it ecologically intelligent? Is it fair? And, is it fun? In an address to Bioneers 2000 in Ukiah, California William McDonough equated these three additional design criteria to life, liberty and the pursuit of happiness.[11] Sounds a bit like a Bill of Rights doesn't it? Maybe this is a bill of rights for environmental design? In the same speech he mentions that his design team constantly asks themselves two additional questions. How do we love all of the children of all species for all time? And, when do we become native to this place? Both of these questions are linked together in the Native American attitude that we are borrowing this earth from our children. If our design work is making the future less for our children or less for the children of the sparrows that live in the elm tree outside our windows, then we have not been successful as designers. For many years now the indigenous peoples of the world have been an historical model of people that knew how to live in harmony with our environment. We value their connection to the earth and wish that we could do the same. We see ourselves as visitors in our own land. When will we become natives? Only when we are no longer visitors, but connected to and a part of, the total environment will we become natives.

[11]McDonough, William. (2000). *Designing the Next Industrial Revolution*. A lecture given at the Bioneers 2000 conference in Ukiah, California.

# Chapter 3
## Contributions by Environmental Designers to the Balance of Nature

Now that we have presented some of the broader ideas and criteria for sustainability, we should look at some specific things that environmental designers can and cannot do to impact our environment. The sustainability movement is quickly moving away from being a "movement" and is evolving toward being completely imbedded into the everyday processes in environmental design. "Green Building" is still something that needs to be sold to some owners but many, more enlightened owners are insisting that their projects be sustainable. It saves them money in the long run and many of their customers are now insisting on it.

## WHAT CAN BE DONE BY ENVIRONMENTAL DESIGNERS

Carbon reduction in the environment is essential to reversing global warming. The following list includes a set of strategies for reducing carbon in our environment. The list also includes strategies that save energy or reduce waste, each of which also impact the release of carbon into the atmosphere. Each strategy is something that is controlled or significantly impacted by environmental designers.

- Reduce the use of automobiles—each mile not driven saves one pound of carbon.
  - Plan more walkable communities thereby reducing the reliance on the automobile.
  - Plan, support and build a transit system in every city.
  - Make the pedestrian the top priority in planning and urban design.
  - Plan and design bicycle networks to connect all neighborhoods.
  - Specify building materials that are available within a short drive, say 500 miles. Shipping costs money and contributes considerably to greenhouse gases.
- Green the environment—each tree planted absorbs one ton of carbon in its lifetime.
  - Create landscaped paths that connect the centers of all neighborhoods in the city.
  - Create interior plantscapes that provide oxygen for the inhabitants, filter the air, and capture carbon.
  - Plan for new forests and recreation areas, make national parks for carbon capture and oxygen production.
- Reduce emissions beyond automobiles.
  - Use alternative energy sources for all buildings—buildings should generate power beyond what they consume.

- Eliminate burning of any consumables for heating which could eliminate carbon emissions from all buildings.
- Specify building materials that minimize off-gassing and that eliminate toxic off-gassing.

- Reduce energy consumption.
  - Daylight every part of every building.
  - Change to energy efficient light sources for artificial lighting. Changing one incandescent light bulb to a compact fluorescent bulb saves 150 pounds of carbon a year.
  - Decrease the amount of hot water used.
  - Install automatic energy shut-offs for unoccupied spaces.
  - Natural ventilation should be included in every building.

- Reduce the amount of water being consumed and polluted.
  - Design and create grey water systems. Grey water is the water that has been used in sinks or baths that can be easily filtered and used to water plants or flush toilets, etc.
  - Use potable water only for human and animal consumption, not for watering plants or for industrial processes.
  - Capture and use rain water and snow melt.
  - Create natural wetland water cleaning areas.

- Eliminate waste from the built environment.
  - Recycle everything used in buildings.

# WHAT CANNOT BE DONE BY ENVIRONMENTAL DESIGNERS

Environmental designers have influence on a great number of people and control over many decisions that impact our planet's sustainability. We do not, however, control many of the most important aspects of sustainability.

## Broad-Based Efforts

- Set aggressive, meaningful and mandatory international limits on the production of greenhouse gases. Limits that will get us to an emission level of one-third of the 1990 level. That is a 66% global reduction not a 5% reduction.

- Implement true cost of products. The cost of many products, if not most, do not reflect the total cost of producing and disposing of the product. If we had to pay for the cost of pollution clean-up in the cost of a product we might not be able to afford the product. One way or another society ends up paying for the total costs of products—right now those costs are not associated with the individual products. One great set of examples are the thousands of industrial sites that are contaminated with heavy metals, poisons, petroleum, etc. all over the developed world. The United States government has had to tax all of us to create a super-fund to pay billions of dollars to clean up this pollution left by industry.

- Develop alternative fuels for individual mobility.

- Develop alternative materials that do not use non-renewable resources. We can help or support this by specifying materials that are made from re-cycled, re-used, or renewable sources.

- Plan for and create new forests and recreation areas that are protected as national forests for the specific purpose of creating oxygen and capturing carbon.

- Change industry to eliminate waste. Develop new materials and processes that can re-use outdated or worn out materials at the same level of quality as the original material allowing it to be recycled indefinitely. I would recommend reading William McDonough and Michael Brangart's book *Cradle to Cradle: Remaking the Way We Make Things* for some really incredible ideas and examples of new materials and industrial processes. It is their position that eliminating waste from our processes makes sense for sustainability, but also makes economic sense for the companies involved.

- Look to nature to develop alternative fertilizers and pesticides for agriculture.

## Individual Efforts by Others
### (including personal efforts of environmental designers)

These are things that the environmentalists have been talking about for years and years and they are still valid today. It is very difficult to create social change. The only way it happens is through individual change; lots and lots of individual change.

- Control the population.

- Adjust thermostats: 2° up in summer and 2° down in winter will eliminate one ton of carbon from the atmosphere.

- Cut down the consumables you purchase, reduce the garbage you create, avoid packaging: a 10% reduction in garbage per person per year will save one-half ton of carbon per person from going into the atmosphere.

- Turn off electrical devices when not in use.

- Buy an electric car. General Motors can't stop the development of effective electric cars forever. See the film *Who Killed the Electric Car* by Chris Paine for some insights into the challenges faced by people that would like to make substantive changes in the way we approach the earth and our lives.

This is not an exhaustive list of strategies for creating a sustainable future for our children. It is only a minimal beginning. The environmental design fields are full of wonderfully creative people that will find many more ways to lead us to a sustainable future. If you would like to make a suggestion send it to me at Don.Faulkner@ndsu.edu. I would appreciate being able to include more ideas in this book in future years.

# PART 2

# The History and Process of Design

This will not be the typical history of architecture or interior design. There is ample time to study the historical record of designed objects in the coming years. Most universities have excellent art history and architecture history courses that look specifically at the important design developments at any given time in history. There are also many great books on the history of art and architecture. Instead, Part 2 will focus on placing the environmental design history into the larger context of history and to trace the design process through history. In addition to the history contained in Chapter 4, we will start our look into the process of design that is used by all environmental designers.

# *Chapter 4*
# History of Design

David Macaulay, in his book *Motel of the Mysteries* warns us that we have to be very careful how we interpret the evidence of history when we create the stories of past cultures.[1] We really do not know the truth because we were not there. We do the best job that we can to interpret what we see, but we should always keep in mind that it is interpretation.

To look at the history of environmental design we have to fuse together the separate histories of planning, architecture, engineering, landscape architecture, and interior design. I am much more interested in looking at the common themes that run through the combined history than in maintaining, what I think is an artificial distinction between the environmental design fields. As I look back at the history of environmental design, I believe that there are several themes that keep reoccurring throughout history. We seem to be driven by some of these themes or just accept them as an innate part of human nature.

- A need to change.
- A desire for continuity which leads to a cycling of design styles.
- A need to improve and do a better job.
- An innate need to make things more complex.
- A need to create and to evolve technologically.
- A need to build big.
- A need to express the values of the society.
- A desire to increase dignity in the world.

**CHANGE** Our society, and indeed we humans thrive on change. It is always a part of our world. The seasons change. We get older and experience new things. We want to see what is just over that hill. We are driven by change and to change.

**CONTINUITY** To the contrary, we do not like change at all. It is one of the great dichotomies of human existence. We want and need change, but we do not like change and we want some continuity in our lives. We want to know that some things don't change. This dichotomy leads us to move forward in pretty jerky steps. Our society moves ahead two steps and then back one, only to move two steps ahead again and back one again. Environmental designers have reflected this desire for continuity by returning to classical forms again and again after a period of rapid change.

---

[1]Macaulay, David. (1979). *Motel of the Mysteries.* Houghton Mifflin Company, Boston.

**IMPROVEMENT** An overriding human need is to do things better than we did them the last time. We need to improve our lot in life and to make our lives more comfortable. The qualities of the spaces that environmental designers create have improved dramatically over time. We continue to want more and better. This is probably one reason why it is impossible to get people to settle for less. When we have the flexibility and mobility given to us by the car, it is very difficult to get people to give it up, even if the car is compromising our planet.

**COMPLEXITY** Our lives are more complex than ever. Complexity is a theme of life that we seem to have little control over. We are driven to complexity. As we look at architectural styles throughout history they have always started as simple, often elegant ways of approaching design. Over the years the style evolves to become more and more complex until it seems to break under its own weight and designers turn to a new, simpler style or return to a previous simpler style. This complexity dance is just like the change dance in that we may move back on occasion but we continue to create more complex structures with each passing year. All environmental design fields are solving much more complex problems today than they did twenty years ago.

**CREATIVITY AND TECHNOLOGY** Environmental designers, like all artists, have a need to create. It is a drive that is not really understandable; it is just a part of us. Combining disparate elements in new and different ways to solve a problem and build something is a powerful drive. This desire to create helps develop the technology that we seem to enjoy. We love new technology and how it helps us to create new things. Technology has influenced many of the major developments in environmental design. The development of structural steel at the same time as the development of the elevator allowed architects to create skyscrapers. Technology continues to help drive creativity in environmental design and is one of the reasons that society continues to become more complex over time.

**BUILDING BIG** This is a need that we have that is just baffling. We need to build things bigger. We have a desire to build taller, broader, or longer, or all of them at once. Even though we know that bigger is not always better, we still seem to have an historical need to build things larger. We see this throughout history and it doesn't seem to be stopping any time soon.

**SOCIAL EXPRESSION** Environmental designers, just like everybody else, are a product of their time in history. Everybody expresses the values of their society in the things that they do. We really cannot help it. The values expressed by environmental designers in their work may vary from region to region around the world but they are a reflection of the time and place of the designer. Even when a designer tries to copy the style or feel of the past they do so with an unmistakable pastiche of the present. Environmental designers create a great deal of what we use to judge a culture. The remnants of ancient buildings and cities and gardens provide insight into the people that created them.

**DIGNITY** The need to continually move toward dignity is an idea from Dr. Jennifer James. She observed that our society has been evolving over history to constantly improve the way that we treat each other. She takes pains to point out that this movement is even more jerky than our technological improvement or our overall process of change. This is a case where we may take two steps forward and one and three-quarter steps back. This progress is slow but we strive to treat all people better than we have in the past regardless of race, beliefs, gender, and sexual preference. As environmental designers we see this in the way that we now accommodate handicapped individuals. We also see it in the way we design healing gardens and memorials to past peoples. Hopefully the current trend toward sustainability is an extension of this move toward dignity as we begin the realize that we must treat the earth and all of its processes with equal dignity.

These various themes have been consistent throughout history. They are at play in all of our work today. Figure 2.1 shows a timeline of environmental design history that traces these themes. The changes occur more and more quickly as we get closer to our own time. It is indeed getting very complicated to design today. Projects are highly complex, large, and demand more and more of the designers. Change is happening very quickly.

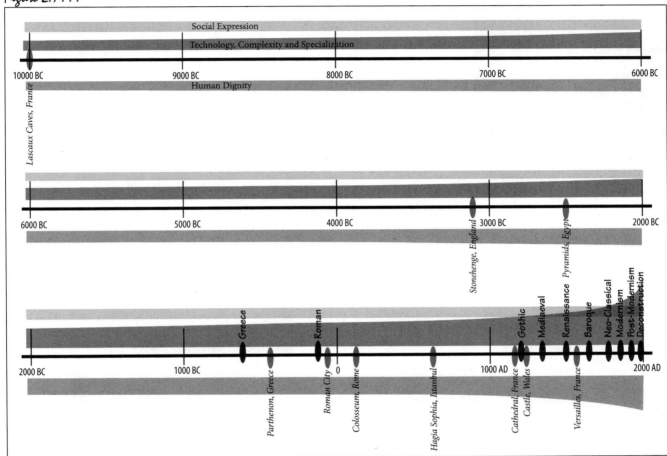

A timeline of environmental design history and the themes we rely on.

As we look at the timeline we begin to understand that development and change were very slow for thousands and thousands of years. We learned significant things about building and agriculture, but the knowledge was simple enough that everyone had the knowledge and the ability to use it. We learned from each other. Knowledge was passed down from generation to generation. If one person exercised their creativity and improved their plantings or their building, they could pass that knowledge on. If they failed at an improvement, they could also pass that knowledge along. We built cities without the help of professional designers. We call this type of design "vernacular" design. Vernacular is defined as: "of, relating to, or being the common building style of a period or place."[2] Before the need to specialize in the environmental design fields, buildings were built in a piece-meal way.

[2]Mish, Frederick C. ed. (1993). *Merriam-Webster's Collegiate Dictionary, Tenth Edition*. Merriam-Webster, Incorporated, Springfield, MA. Page 1312.

Figure 2.2 . . .

Vernacular construction in the city of York, England. Vernacular cities were built as the need arose with the technology of the day and local materials.

The skills and expertise were passed from neighbor to neighbor or father to son. If someone was in need of a new house they would build it right next to an existing home using one of the existing walls as a common wall. It would also be built exactly like the adjacent home in construction and materials. In this way the cities grew in a very organic way, one piece at a time.

As society developed new technology, built bigger, and started to get more complex, we began to specialize in the type of work we did. People began to amass specialized knowledge as quarrymen, stone cutters, carvers, metal workers, etc. In addition to the skilled craftsmen, there was a need for people that knew how to envision the entire project and how to organize the work. Maybe it was to build the pyramids (around 2500 BC) or maybe it was something even before that, but the person that created the overall vision for the pyramid and had the knowledge to level the site, orient the new structure to the cardinal directions and organize the specialized workers and the laborers, became one of the first environmental designers.

Figure 2.3 . . .

Stonehenge, Salisbury Plain in England.

Figure 2.4 . . .

A detail of the stones at Stonehenge.

Prior to the building of the pyramids in Egypt, around 3000 BC, construction was begun on a henge in the Salisbury Plains of southern England. Someone had to conceive of the idea of a henge. Henges are typically a round structure that had specific orientation to the seasonal solstices and equinoxes. They were used to acknowledge the importance of the seasons to agriculture, and to worship the gods associated with growing and the harvest. (You will notice that we are into one of the stories of past cultures that I mentioned earlier with the caution from *Motel of the Mysteries*.) We really don't know if this is the correct use for the henges but the evidence points in this direction. Part of the importance of henges or other constructions like them, is that they represent communal building for a purpose beyond the day to day. This is building as a social expression not as a necessity. The earliest henges were earthworks, circular banks, ditches and mounds. We might think of the people that envisioned the earthworks as the first landscape architects. Early henges often had structures made of wood or possibly reeds or other grown materials. The evidence of their existence is very minimal because the materials used have degraded and disappeared over the years. The only physical remains are holes in the ground that could have had wood poles in them. The tradition of the henge was passed down from generation to generation or from tribe to tribe. In the process of expanding the henge at Salibury, someone, whom we might call an early environmental designer, envisioned the henge built of more permanent materials. The henge was added to in stone which gives the henge its name, Stonehenge. A little more about what we know and don't know about Stonehenge. We know it is there. We know where the stones were quarried. The blue stones are the shorter ones in an inner ring. They are about six feet tall and came from Wales, some 240 miles away. We have no idea how the stones were moved from Wales to Salisbury. The tall stones and lintels, were brought from Marlborough Downs about 20 miles north of Stonehenge. Each of the uprights weighs about 25 tons and each lintel (horizontal beam on top of the uprights) weighs about 7 tons. The lintels are notched together and sit on a pin on the top of the uprights to hold them in place. We have no idea how the stones were stood upright or how the stone beams were lifted into place; however, there are several fascinating theories.[3]

As society developed and became more specialized and more organized, the demand for people with knowledge in building our world became more intense. The Greeks (around 400 BC) developed a very sophisticated system of design rules for their temples (see Part 5) and began to develop specialized districts within their cities for worship, trade, and governance. The Romans evolved into an even more complex social structure which demanded more sophisticated, larger and more specialized buildings, interiors and cities. They started to plan cities prior to building them as they expanded into much of present day Europe. The Romans even established a city on the site of London, they called it Londinium. To protect their isolated city they built a wall around it. Parts of that wall are still visible.

Figure 2.5 . . .

Roman Wall in London. The protective wall built around the Roman city of Londinium.

The Romans (around 50 AD) also developed the technology of the arch. This gave them the ability to build larger structures that enclosed more space. This also increased the level of knowledge required of their environmental designers. They also developed concrete and engineered roads that still exist today.

The technology of the arch spread around the world and around 600 AD the cathedral of Hagia Sophia was built in Istanbul, Turkey. The arches and domes were magnificent and existed to praise God by getting the people closer to God in their worship spaces. The church has served that purpose ever since, first as a Christian Cathedral and now as a Muslim Mosque.

This tendency to build bigger and bigger churches, as an expression of the society's focus on religion, continued unabated for centuries. The gothic cathedrals of France and England are monuments to the technology of the arch, the vault, and the dome. Designers were asked to build larger, more elaborate, more light-filled spaces in celebration of the people's relationship with their god. As the complexity increased and the technology evolved,

[3]Osborne, Ken. (1995). *Stonehenge and Neighbouring Monuments*. English Heritage, Westerham Press, London, England.

*Figure 2.6 . . .*

Canterbury Cathedral in Southern England. Reaching as close to heaven as possible.

*Figure 2.7 . . .*

King Henry VII's Chapel at Westminster Abbey in London. Notice the abundance of natural light and the intricacy of the stone arches and vaults.

workers became more and more specialized. Stone masons, carpenters, metal smiths, and many other craftspeople were necessary to complete the projects.

In mediaeval times the social focus shifted slightly away from the church to the more secular. The kings and lords of the land were building castles and towns to solidify their claim to the land and its wealth. These massive and fortified buildings often had towns associated with them that needed the protection of earthworks, walls and gates. Another example of designers with specific knowledge beginning to emerge.

There is evidence of people occupying the area around York, England since the Bronze Age (2000–500 BC). Its settlement as a city was secured when the Romans established Eboracum on the north side of the River Ouse in the first century AD. In the early eleventh century York was the site of numerous wars between the Vikings, the Saxons, and the Normans. Eventually, William the Conqueror, a Norman King, took control of the area and built a castle to control the confluence of the Ouse and Foss Rivers (1068). His castle, now known as Clifford's Tower, was built on a very large artificial earth mound called a motte. It was also surrounded by a water-filled moat connected to the rivers. Clifford's Tower, (Figure 2.8) was a stone replacement for the wood castle. The stone structure was started around 1245 and took twenty years to build.[4] Around the same time a protective wall for the city was constructed utilizing several of the physical features of the Roman fortifications. This type of mediaeval town building was common and required people with a great deal of experience in fortification design, people that probably traveled and saw first hand examples in other parts of Europe.

[4]Butler, Lawrence. Jeffrey, Kate, ed. (1997). *Clifford's Tower and the Castles of York*. English Heritage, London, England.

*Figure 2.8 . . .*

Clifford's Tower on its motte in York, England.

Change in the built environment was still pretty slow as we approached the Renaissance. As you could see above, it took almost two hundred years to replace a wood castle with a stone castle and twenty years to build the relatively modest stone castle. The speed of change was not fast by our standards but had become much faster than it had been in previous history. The Renaissance marked a return to the classical lessons of Greece and Rome and to the preeminence of the church in society. We moved from a simplified approach to building to a more exuberant approach during the Baroque period. Many of the resources of society were split between the church and the monarchies ruling at the time.

Churches again, became bigger and more elaborate but so did buildings and gardens for the aristocracy. Louis XIV, King of France grew tired of the royal palace in Paris and converted his father's hunting lodge in Versailles to the seat of the French government. The palace grew and grew as did the enormous gardens that Louis loved. The work required yet another increase in the specialization of environmental designers as le Notré was charged with creating a vast vision for the gardens at Versailles. Whether he was the first landscape architect or not, it is clear that he filled all of the roles of the modern landscape architect.

The interiors at Versailles were also incredibly complex and involved accommodating the pomp and ceremony of the

*Figure 2.9 . . .*

The York city wall near Bootham Bar, one of the original Roman gates into the city.

*Figure 2.10 . . .*

The Orangerie at the Gardens of Versailles.

*Figure 2.11 . . .*

The Colonnade at the Gardens of Versailles.

*Figure 2.12 . . .*

One of the bedrooms at Versailles showing the elaborate painting and decorating of the walls and ceilings.

Figure 2.13 . . .

The Hall of Battles at Versailles showing the huge paintings of French war victories along the very long walk to visit with the king.

French government. The Hall of Battles was designed to awe and humble visiting state dignitaries as they walked its huge length to have an audience with the king.

The Renaissance lasted over 300 years while the Baroque period lasted some 200 years. Between 1800 AD and the year 2000 we have been through three separate design periods: the Neo-Classical, the Victorian, and now the Modern age. The pace of change has definitely increased. Today, it could be argued, we have three separate styles being pursued: modernism, post-modernism, and deconstruction. Each of them uses all of the most up-to-date technology and works on extremely complex buildings and spaces. Post-modernism is a type of neo-classical revival but it now exists right along side modernism and deconstructionism. Deconstruction adopts a particular social attitude that questions the rules we have come to use in design. Shown below is a recent example of each of these styles of environmental design.

Figure 2.14 . . .

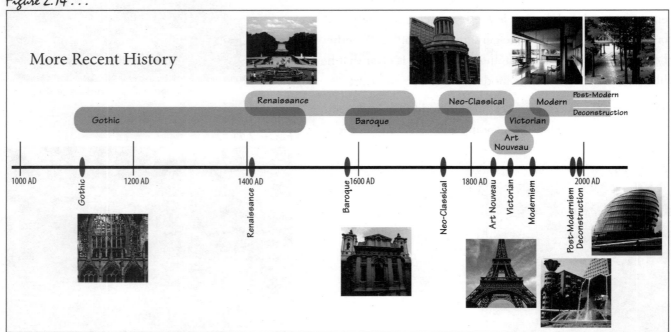

An expanded timeline of the later developments in environmental design.

Figure 2.15...

The straightforward modernism of Machado and Silvetti at the Utah Museum of Fine Art on the campus of the University of Utah.

Figure 2.16...

The post-modern historicism of the city of Celebration in Florida.

Figure 2.17...

The deconstructivist layering of design intention at Parc de la Villette in Paris.

Each of these projects has required a team of environmental designers to complete the projects. The lone-wolf designer is ceasing to exist. There is just too much information for one person to know to be able to do the type of job that is necessary. Environmental design is a highly creative field that now relies on the creativity of a team not just one person.

To close this very cursory look at environmental design history I would like to peer into the future a little bit. By looking at the complexity of the problems for environmental designers, we can reinforce the idea that environmental design needs to be an integrated set of fields, all working for a common set of goals. The following chart looks at the complexity of environmental design projects in mediaeval times, in the 1980's and in the near future.

| **Mediaeval** | **1980's** | **Near Future** |
| --- | --- | --- |
| Natural ventilation | Artificial ventilation | Combination ventilation |
| Mostly natural lighting | Mostly artificial lighting | Combination lighting |
| Minimal heat control | Specific heat control | Specific heat control |
| General space uses | Specialized space uses | Flexible space uses |
| Yell to neighbors | Instant global communication | Instant global communication |
| Pollution impacts local | Pollution impacts globe | Pollution only impacts local |
| Local materials | Materials from anywhere | Regional materials |
| Low energy use | Massive energy use | Sustainable energy use |

Since the things that are mentioned in the future column are beginning to be expectations now, I am hopeful that the future will be within the next three years. Many of the responses listed in the "near future" column look like a return to mediaeval times. They are not. We must look at the much more complex combined systems of nature and our artificial systems. We must combine these systems to create sustainable environments for everyone. Understanding the relationships between our actions and the natural systems that support us is a very new area of knowledge for environmental designers. The new direction makes this a particularly exciting time to be in environmental design.

# The Process of Design

We will look at some basic strategies and activities for designers in Part 4 of this book. Here I would like to review some of our understanding of design as a creative process. Environmental designers use design as a process for solving problems. Design is certainly not the only process for solving problems. The scientific process is well understood as a way to seek the truth by asking a particular question, proposing an answer, and testing the proposed answer. The scientific process has provided us with tremendous advancement in technology, medicine, biology, astro-physics, to name a few. The scientific process works best when it is seeking the truth; something that is provable.

Design, on the other hand, is a process that seeks to find solutions to problems that do not have a specific or correct answer. There are many, many potential solutions to the problems that environmental designers tackle. Certainly, some solutions are better than others, but there is no single correct solution. Environmental design problems are further complicated by the inclusion of human desire, social pressure, aesthetics and emotion into the consideration of the solutions. An environmental design solution arrived at in one culture might be totally inappropriate in another culture. We can also be guaranteed that whatever design solution is executed, not everyone will agree that it is the right solution. Strong opinions about our creations just come with the nature of the work. It takes a certain personal passion to take on design challenges. It also takes a certain acceptance of the chaotic process and the myriad opinions, desires, and emotions tied to design problems.

I would never want to imply that scientists are not passionate about their work or that there are not very strong opinions about the work and how it is done. The difference lies in the end purpose. Science is looking for the correct answer, design is looking for one great solution among many possible ones.

Good design is imbued with the human spirit. It is emotional, and poetic, and linked to our natural environment. Great design also functions. It solves the problems it was asked to solve and it allows for future uses. Great design lasts for a long, long time. It has structural and material quality that lets it age gracefully and effectively. Marcus Vitruvius Polio set three conditions for architecture. I will extend this definition to all of environmental design. Vitruvius said that architecture must have commitas, firmitas and venustas. Architecture, and by extension environmental design, should have the qualities of commodity, firmness and delight. The quality of commodity involves the functioning of the spaces. Design solves problems for human inhabitants. Good environmental design should function well and do so in a way that does not negatively impact life for other inhabitants of this earth. The quality of firmness relates to the long term viability of the project. Firmness means that the quality of materials and construction will last for hundreds of years. Clearly not all buildings, interiors or landscapes provide firmness that will last centuries. All projects should be striving for these goals. Venustas (delight) means that a project should delight the senses. It should be beautiful and magical. It should move us emotionally. Some design projects may actually need to shock us or frighten us, but all projects should move us in some way. The purpose of the Holocaust Museum is not to delight us but to shock us and remind us of the atrocities that mankind has been involved with. It is not possible for an environmental design project to have all of these qualities unless the designer is considering all of these characteristics as they design.

Figure 2.18 . . .

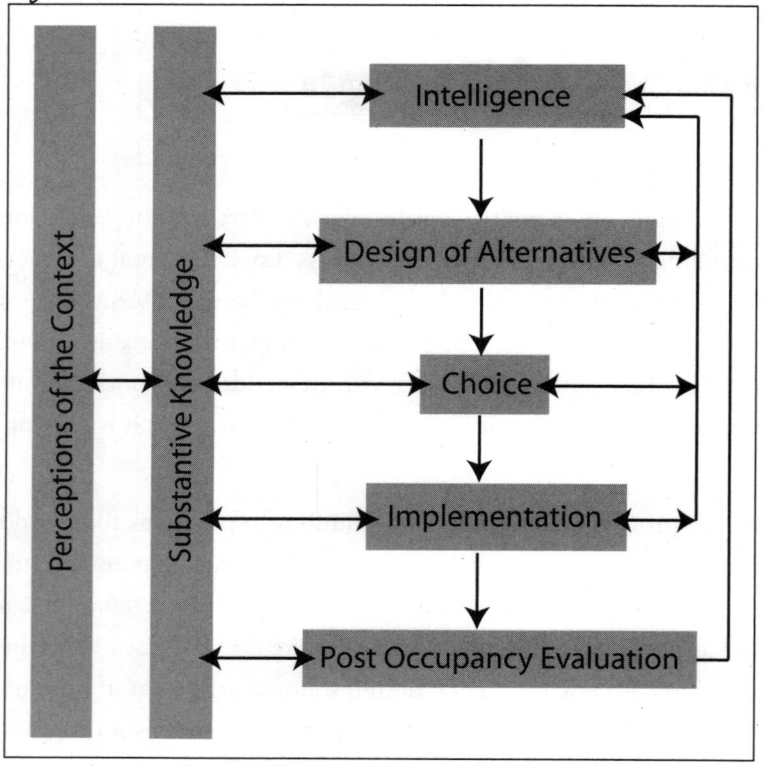

A diagram of a simplified design process as studied by psychologists.

Over the years scientists, mostly psychologists, have studied the process of design to try to understand its intricacies and its success as a problem-solving strategy.

This fairly simple diagram of the design process acknowledges the importance of the context and our human perceptions of that context. It also acknowledges the amassed body of knowledge that environmental design has accumulated over many centuries. The diagram shows a fairly common conception of problem solving within the design process. Starting with the gathering of information (the INTELLIGENCE box on the chart), about the project the designer will then explore a host of DESIGN ALTERNATIVES. Through the development and analysis of many DESIGN ALTERNATIVES we may discover that we need additional knowledge in order to solve the problem. That will take us back to the INTELLIGENCE phase of the process. At some point the designer will CHOOSE a solution from the many explored as the best one to pursue for the project. The designer will then proceed to IMPLEMENT the solution by preparing the documents and descriptions necessary to have the project built. The designer will also work to make sure that the IMPLEMENTATION will be accomplished the way that it had been planned. POST OCCUPANCY EVALUATION refers to a critique of the project after it is completed and after it has been used for a period of time. Designers can learn a great deal about the successes and failures of their work by performing POST OCCUPANCY EVALUATIONS. This step relays information back to our body of knowledge and informs the INTELLIGENCE phase of the next project. You will notice that the diagram indicates that designers might continue to move back and forth between the phases of the project. The designer may be confronted with developments in the implementation phase, might challenge some of the choices that they made and require them to look for more information, try new alternatives and develop a new choice. This would appear to be a linear process—but design is never a linear process.

Figure 2.19 . . .

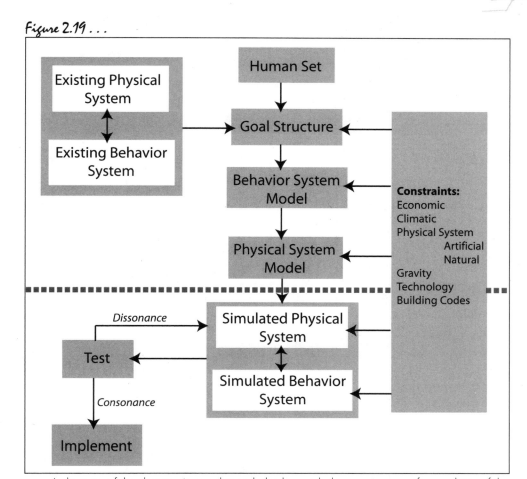

A diagram of the design process that includes human behavior as a specific condition of the design process. Diagram adapted from Studer (1969).

The diagram above maps the design process with a different viewpoint. This diagram looks very specifically at the inclusion of human behavior in the design process. We can see that there are two groups of knowledge; EXISTING PHYSICAL SYSTEM knowledge and EXISTING BEHAVIOR SYSTEM knowledge both contribute to the formation of the goals of the project. This diagram is important not only because it includes human behavior in our process but because it acknowledges the importance of setting the goals for the project. Many times the formulation of the goals for the project is the most important task that a designer will undertake. If there is no clear understanding of the problem and what the goals are for its solution, we don't have much of a chance to solve the problem. We can lay this diagram on top of the previous one and include everything above the dotted line into the intelligence phase. Human behavior does need to be considered when designing within our environment. The SIMULATED PHYSICAL and BEHAVIOR SYSTEMS exist for every design alternative that we explore. The decision process, choosing the best design alternative, then includes a much deeper understanding of the behavior systems that we expect within the new environment, and whether they are compatible with the goals of the project.

For future environmental designers I would like to add an additional system to this model. In order to create sustainable design solutions I would like to add "Natural Systems" both existing and simulated to this diagram. If we were looking at the physical, behavioral, and natural systems for each project we could be doing better, more sustainable design work.

Figure 2.20 . . .

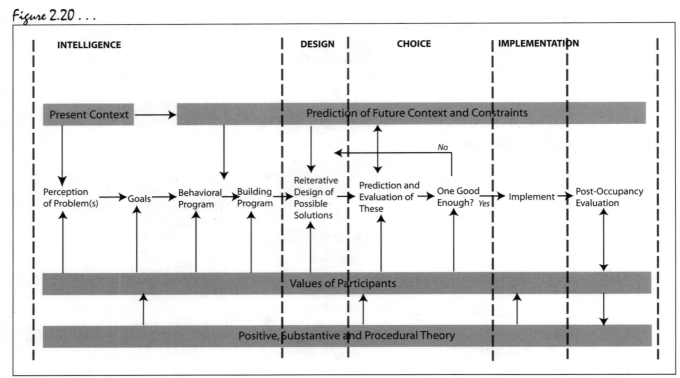

A more complete diagram of the design process.

Here we see a diagram with the now familiar design phases across the top of the chart. We also see both the PRESENT CONTEXT and a PREDICTION OF FUTURE CONTEXT AND CONSTRAINTS. It is here that we could include the consequences and constraints placed on our work by the natural environment and our desire to be sustainable. Along the bottom we see the consideration of the VALUES OF PARTICIPANTS. The opinions, emotions, dreams, desires, and values of clients and the public are important to any environmental design project. The bottom bar in the chart refers to the body of knowledge that we have in the field. The important distinction here is that it is described as POSITIVE, SUBSTANTIVE AND PROCEDURAL THEORY. This is the basic knowledge that underlies our many rules. This is the difference between knowing the building code related to fire exits and knowing how people will instinctively react in a fire situation. The only problem in the diagram is that it indicates a linear process from perception of the problem to implementation and post-occupancy evaluation. As mentioned above, the design process is never a linear process. I would suggest the following change to the diagram shown on the following page.

None of these diagrams really help our understanding of the process that is at the center of each of the diagrams. The exploration of design alternatives may as well be a black box in the middle of these diagrams. There is no description of the processes, the tools used, or the products generated as design alternatives are evaluated and analyzed. To many people, the activity of design exploration is a magical process. It is hard to describe. It is even harder to diagram. It is hard to show. It is indeed one of those things that must be experienced to truly be understood. That is why the education systems for environmental design is studio based. Design education is about doing the work of design. Environmental design students learn by practicing design. It is about asking the big questions that need to be answered in our society and about exploring the possibilities for their solution.

Figure 2.21 . . .

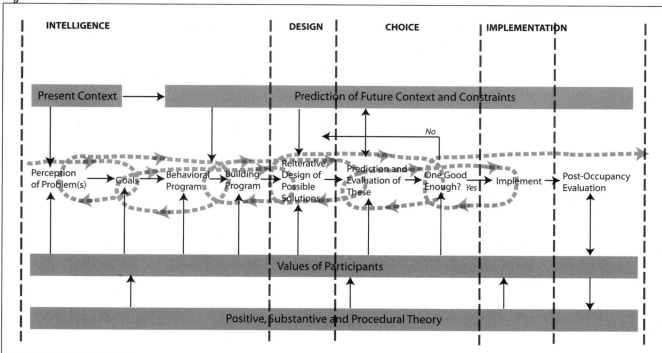

My variation of the design process diagram.

It is easy to show the results of the design process. The results include cities, and town squares, and parks, and gardens, and buildings, and interior spaces. We can go visit them and take pictures of them as we wander around in them. We can evaluate them directly, based on our first hand experience. Creating and evaluating design possibilities is a bit more difficult. It does involve a long, involved process observing and documenting the existing conditions and getting tuned into the physical, natural and emotional context of the place. It involves proposing possible solutions and exploring them through drawings, paintings, models, sculptures, diagrams and virtual simulations. Through this exploration we can evaluate the efficacy of each possible solution or each part of the many solutions. This exploration is the part of design that most people do not see. They often are unaware of the hundreds or thousands of man-hours that go into understanding the problem and exploring the potential of the problem. On the following pages are a few examples of the objects that are developed and the tools used in the exploration of some environmental design problems. Each example is from work done by environmental design students at North Dakota State University in the spring semester of 2007.

Figure 2.22 . . .

A napkin sketch of an existing urban scene in San Francisco.

Figure 2.23 . . .

A napkin sketch of some design possibilities.

Figure 2.24 . . .

A collage exploring the physical features and the emotional response to an urban setting.

Figure 2.25 . . .

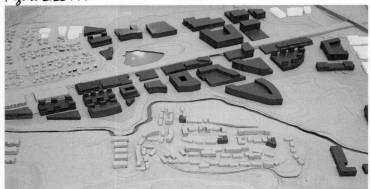

A model illustrating the context of an urban design problem. The model will be used to test alternate solutions for the project.

Figure 2.26 . . .

A section through a lake and a hill exploring some possible approaches to designing the new landscape.

Figure 2.27 . . .

A painting exploring the form and activity of a proposed environmental design project.

Figure 2.28 . . .

An concept model looking at an abstract approach to an architectural problem.

*Figure 2.29 . . .*

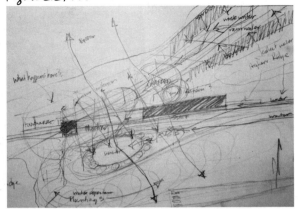

An early plan sketch for one possible solution to an environmental design problem.

*Figure 2.30 . . .*

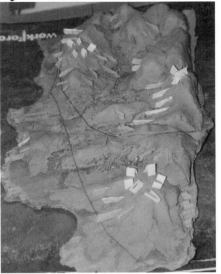

A model of a proposed solution for a landscape architecture project.

*Figure 2.31 . . .*

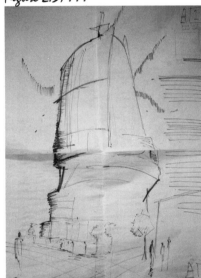

A large perspective sketch of a potential solution for a high-rise building. The sketch is about four feet tall.

*Figure 2.32 . . .*

Several quick model proposals for the same high-rise building project.

*Figure 2.33 . . .*

Another potential solution for a high-rise, mixed use building.

Figure 2.34 . . .

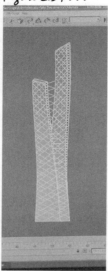

A computer model (virtual model) of the same project shown in Figure 2.33.

Figure 2.35 . . .

A working model to explore the interior design options of a major public space at the base of a high-rise building.

Figure 2.36 . . .

A model used to explore the details of a building entrance.

Figure 2.37 . . .

A presentation model prepared for entry into an architectural design competition.

These illustrations give you a small insight into the types of products and explorations an environmental designer might use in the design process. What these examples can't tell you is the nature of the problem being investigated. They can't show the threads of thought and emotion that link these design notions to the problem, the context and the future.

# PART 3

# The Disciplines of Environmental Design

*A*fter the discussion about a united environmental design field, it seems somewhat hypocritical to now talk about the various environmental design disciplines separately. Each of the fields that we consider to be a part of environmental design are separately licensed to practice, and each requires a separate and distinct path through education and internship. I would hope that eventually we will see all of the environmental design fields merge into a single discipline with sub-specialties, much like medicine. It would be a more accurate reflection of the way that the environmental disciplines combine to impact the environment and our society. We would all do a better job if we shared a basic language and understood each other's points of view.

The environmental fields that we will investigate more fully here will be Planning, Urban Design, Landscape Architecture, Architecture, Engineering and Interior Design. They are being presented from the largest scale of work to the smallest. Professionals in each of these distinctive disciplines take leadership positions in projects within their own realm. Each may also act as consultants to the other environmental designers on any given project. Each of these fields sees itself as having distinctive areas of work. Each of these fields also recognizes significant areas of overlap in their work.

Figure 3.1 shows the relationship of the various environmental design disciplines to each other. It indicates the size, or scale, of projects undertaken by each discipline; examples of possible design projects at each scale and an indication of the overlap between the disciplines. The overlap between disciplines is substantial and occasionally causes ill feelings or even legal action when one discipline believes that another is practicing within their world of work.

*Figure 3.1 . . .*

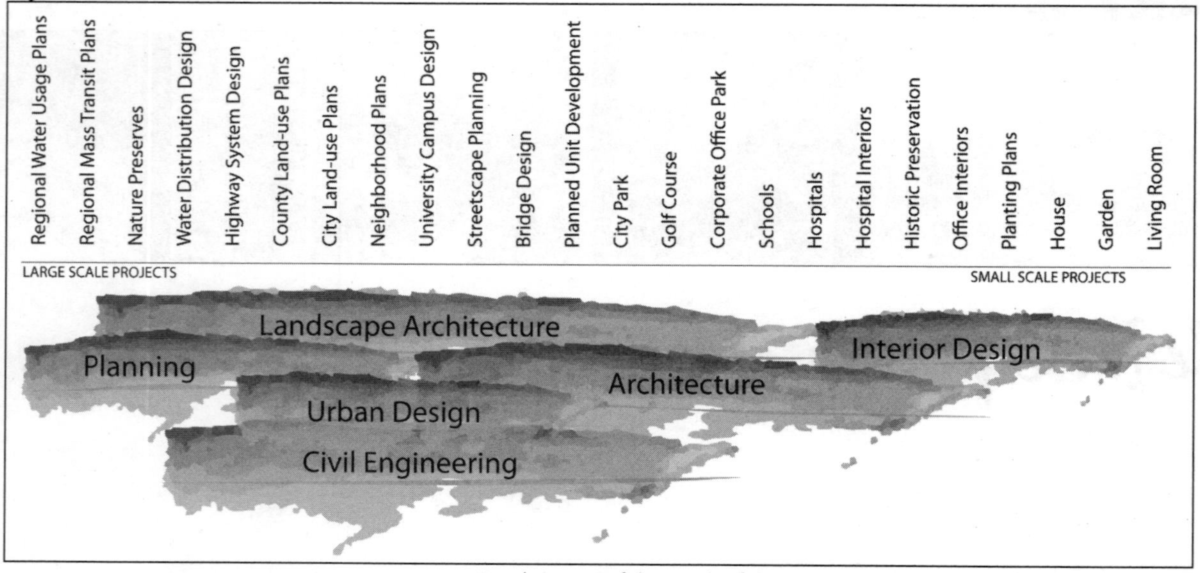

Large scale projects (left) to small scale projects (right):
Regional Water Usage Plans · Regional Mass Transit Plans · Nature Preserves · Water Distribution Design · Highway System Design · County Land-use Plans · City Land-use Plans · Neighborhood Plans · University Campus Design · Streetscape Planning · Bridge Design · Planned Unit Development · City Park · Golf Course · Corporate Office Park · Schools · Hospitals · Hospital Interiors · Historic Preservation · Office Interiors · Planting Plans · House · Garden · Living Room

LARGE SCALE PROJECTS — SMALL SCALE PROJECTS

Planning · Landscape Architecture · Urban Design · Civil Engineering · Architecture · Interior Design

Overlapping of the work of the various environmental design disciplines.

It is impossible to talk about one field of environmental design without talking about several others at the same time. The linkages, overlaps, and interrelatedness of the work shows up over and over again. It is this inter-connectedness that I wish to highlight. The close ties between each of the environmental design disciplines leads me to wish for a more comprehensive approach and an end to the distinctions between the fields. I am sure that it will be very obvious as you read about each of the environmental design fields that the overlap is substantial and unavoidable. In fact, I believe it is desirable.

# Planning

Planning is the environmental design field that deals with the largest scale of projects. There are several different types of planners, among them regional planners, city planners, environmental planners, recreation planners and transportation planners. The scale of their work involves areas such as geographic regions, cities, counties or neighborhoods.

The work of planners involves the physical environment that we live within, but it also extends into realms that do not involve the physical nature of places. Planners also work in areas such as health care planning, social services planning, economic development, crime prevention, and other realms that do not have direct bearing on the physical nature of our environment. These types of planners have much more to do with the social and economic nature of our society. Our discussions here will be somewhat limited to those planners that deal with our physical environment, such as city planners.

Planning is philosophically focused on creating the best environments for the largest numbers of people in as egalitarian a way as possible. Much of the work involves the creation of rules and regulations that help to insure equal treatment of all people and a healthy environment for everyone. Because much of the focus of planning is on creating rules and enforcing them, planners are the most bureaucratic group within environmental design. Planners are also involved with the public in ways that most of the other design fields are not. Planners are often engaged with large groups of people that are interested in the quality of their living and working environments or with people that will be affected by the work being contemplated. It takes a particular set of skills and a particular patience to be a great planner.

Many planners work within the public realm, working for city planning offices or state planning offices or regional government planning offices. A fairly large number of planners work as private consultants for government or private agencies, and companies working on a project by project basis. Some planners work in multi-discipline design firms, with other environmental designers, providing services to clients also on a project by project basis. The advantage of a multi-discipline firm should be clear as we continue to explore the amount of overlap between all of the environmental design fields.

## REGIONAL PLANNING

Regional planners are concerned with the functioning of environmental systems as they affect large, multi-jurisdictional regions. The regions that they deal with are often related to larger geographic areas such as watersheds. There have been recommendations, in the past, that the twelve major river drainages in the United States are the best way for us to look at regional planning. The Tennessee Valley Authority was established in 1933 by the federal government to help deal with the devastated landscape and economy of the Tennessee River Valley. The Tennessee Valley Authority (TVA) was charged with providing flood protection, navigation and generation of electricity within the Tennessee River drainage which included Tennessee and parts of Kentucky, North Carolina, Georgia, Alabama and Mississippi. Over the years this highly influential and successful regional planning authority extended their work to include reforestation, soil conservation, outdoor recreation, community building, manufacturing of fertilizers, and the retirement of marginal farm land.[1]

The work of regional planners has always been very important, but as our population continues to increase and our demand for water and other resources increases along with that population, our regional planners will have a particular burden placed on them to find and solve resource problems for very large numbers of people. The sustainability of our development patterns is of major concern to regional planners.

One example of the important nature of regional planning is the availability of water for the Los Angeles basin. The city of Los Angeles gets a great deal of its drinking and irrigation water from the Colorado River system. The Colorado River system drains some 244,000 square miles of Colorado, Utah, Wyoming, Arizona, and Nevada. Two very large dams and reservoirs exist on the Colorado, Glenn Canyon Dam with Lake Powell and Hoover Dam with its associated Lake Mead. Both of these huge reservoirs provide water to the city of Los Angeles and its surrounding area as well as to its own drainage area. The water that is used in Los Angeles is diverted from the natural drainage at Lake Havasoo where it goes into the 242 mile long Colorado River Aqueduct. So much water is used in Southern California and the rest of the drainage, that the Colorado River is just a trickle as it empties into the Gulf of California. The population of the Los Angeles basin is growing rapidly but so are the populations of Utah, Colorado, Arizona and

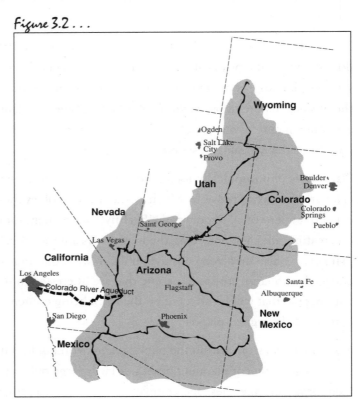

Figure 3.2 . . .

A map of the Colorado River drainage and its pipeline to Los Angeles.

Nevada. In fact, the fastest growing city in the United State is Las Vegas, Nevada. Phoenix has also grown substantially over the last several decades.

Each of these states are demanding additional water resources for agricultural, industrial and residential uses. In 1963 the allocation of water from the Colorado River to the city of Los Angeles was reduced to 4.4 million acre feet of water a year. Their demand continues to exceed 5.2 million acre feet a year. The new agreements also limit the amount of water leaving the Colorado River Basin to extra water not being used within the basin. In recent years Arizona has been using close to their total allocation eliminating any extra water being available for diversion to Los Angeles. The questions is, Where will the additional water come from? The condition in Southern California is duplicated all over the world. It does not take a crystal ball to see that water may be the cause of

[1]Bartuska, Tom J. and Gerald L. Young, ed. *The Built Environment: A Creative Inquiry into Design and Planning*. Crisp Publications, Inc., Menlo Park, CA. 1994. Page 320.

serious conflicts not only in the United States but throughout the world in years to come. The challenge for regional planners has certainly been established. Creative planners will have to develop sustainable strategies that reduce the need for water dramatically, but also develop ways to apply technology and common sense to the distribution of water for our future.

Problems of such a large scale are daunting but they are also exciting to grapple with and to solve. Regional planners must bring the ability to see multiple issues in interrelated ways to their work. It is exciting and important work for our planet.

Regional planners also work within regions that are a bit smaller than the huge watersheds mentioned above. Many regional planners work in transportation looking for solutions to our transportation issues in multi-county areas around major cities. These planners look for strategies that help move people and goods in efficient, cost effective, and energy saving ways throughout our cities and between our cities. Other regional planners may be involved in planning, designing, and maintaining recreation facilities for large, multi-jurisdictional regions. These regional recreation planners are charged with providing a wide variety of opportunities for people's recreation needs throughout large cities. The range of activities that they plan can be substantial and might include organized sports such as baseball, golf, ice hockey; more individual sporting opportunities such as hiking, skiing, swimming and boating; and more passive recreation such as picnicking and sunbathing. The ability for people to be active in the outdoors is an important part of our human existence. Planning for these recreation opportunities provides challenges that are both broad and specific. The Fargo, North Dakota/Moorhead, Minnesota area just hired a bicycle planner to work with community groups to expand and improve the opportunities for bicycling within the metropolitan area. This is a person with a planning background that also has a passion for bicycling and has chosen to specialize in that area.

Figure 3.3 . . .

A bicycle path along the Red River of the North in Fargo, North Dakota.

## PLANNING STRATEGIES AND GEOGRAPHIC INFORMATION SYSTEMS

Regional planners may look at a broad set of goals within a region or may look at a specific set of goals for their region. Regional planners look at the largest scale of projects in environmental design. One of the tasks falling to regional planners may be the determination of the suitability of an area for human development. The pioneering work of Ian L. McHarg as illustrated in his 1967 book *Design With Nature* has become the foundation for many of the sustainable development tools in use today. McHarg developed a design strategy that evaluated potential development sites in many different areas of concern. He would map such concerns as: slope, surface drainage, soil drainage, bedrock foundation, soil foundation, susceptibility to erosion, land values, historic values, water values, scenic values, recreation values, residential values, forest values, wildlife values, institutional values, tidal inundation, flood planes, prime agricultural land, aquifers, aquifer recharge areas, marshes, etc. Each map was produced on a transparent overlay which would allow the planner to combine maps together to find the areas most appropriate for development. The system attempts to find the physical and social value of the land under study and to make sure that development meshes with the natural systems and the social values of the place. This way of looking at planning was a giant leap for the profession.[2]

Today we have computer programs, Geographic Information Systems, that allow us to place the maps and information into a digital form that is easily combined and analyzed. Geographic Information Systems (GIS) have become the backbone of much of the work that is done by planners. Although the amounts of data that are needed to do this type of planning are staggering, it is now possible to accumulate that data and store it so that everyone can have access to it and use it to do a better job of planning. All levels of planning now rely on GIS and must thank Professor McHarg for the work that he pioneered. Our hope is that GIS will increase the amount and value of the information that we have to make the critical decisions of planning.

## CITY PLANNING

City planners have a very interesting job. They must look many years into the future and determine the best set of possibilities for the sustainable growth of their city. This is not an easy job, particularly in the United States where each individual has been raised to believe that they have the right to do whatever they want whenever they want to. This is particularly true when it comes to property that we might own. It has been our collective dream for hundreds of years to own our own piece of the country in order to secure our place in society and in our world. You might imagine that there is some difficulty when a city planner begins to limit what a person might wish to do on their particular piece of property.

Figure 3.4 . . .

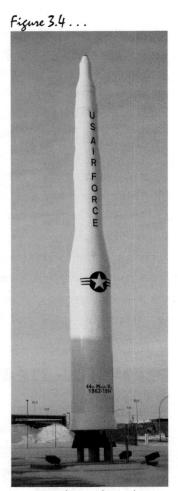

A rocket similar to the one mentioned in the adjacent story.

*One day while driving near the mouth of Little Cottonwood Canyon in suburban Salt Lake City I happened to notice a rocket standing on the top of the hill to my left. This was not a little thing, it was something like a Minute Man Rocket (I really don't know what type of rocket it was) towering some thirty feet into the air. This is not a usual site in the foothills and I certainly was not the only person that noticed it. The news media saw it too and it was indeed a feature item on the news that evening. The property owner had acquired the rocket as surplus somehow and thought that it made a great lawn ornament. The neighbors weren't so sure that it was an appropriate decorative element within their neighborhood. After a great deal of discussion and angst, the property owner was told to remove the rocket from his property and he grudgingly complied.*

[2]McHarg, Ian. *Design With Nature.* (1967, 1992). John Wiley & Sons, Inc. New York.

Planners were involved in this situation because they write the zoning rules which establish the acceptable uses within various areas of the city. This is not a usual situation and the zoning laws did not cover having a missile in your front yard. Zoning codes however, do usually contain passages that prohibit individuals from constructing things on their private property that become a nuisance for other people in the neighborhood. The traffic that this missile was generating already was creating a nuisance. With their charge to protect the health, safety, and welfare of the public, planners must mediate in some very interesting situations when individual desires come in conflict with the good of the public.

The legal justification for planning is contained in the 14th Amendment to the United States Consti-

Figure 3.5...

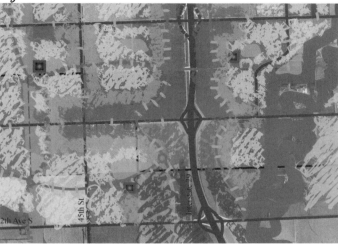

A portion of a municipal land use plan showing lower density residential areas, medium to high density residential areas, commercial areas, parks, schools, and industrial areas. Land use plans are typically in color, which we could not duplicate here.

tution which gives government the ability to control land uses. It also gives government police powers in order to assure public safety. In addition, the 10th Amendment to the United States Constitution gives the government the power of eminent domain. Eminent domain powers allow the government to seize private property as long as the seizure is for the public good. The government cannot just take someone's property, they must compensate the owner at fair market value.

The ability to control land uses as granted by the 14th amendment, is the foundation of planning. The health problems caused when housing was built adjacent to dirty industries during the industrial revolution made it essential that our society be able to control land use. The filth and pollution in which people lived created substantial health problems for the workers and the city at large. Early land use planning tried to resolve these problems by making sure that industry had its own place in the city and that housing was constructed at a safe distance from that industry. City zoning codes are the vehicles used to address these problems of land use and to help assure a safe and healthy city. In addition to establishing the basic land use pattern of the city, planners have been given the task of making sure that the city grows and develops in ways that serve the greatest number of people and that are economically feasible. The operation of a city is a very expensive undertaking; one that planner's impact greatly.

Besides land use, city planners control other aspects of development such as residential density (the number of housing units that can be built on an acre of land), set-back of structures from the property lines, height of buildings, the type and width of streets, the existence of sidewalks, architectural style and materials, even rules about maintenance of private property.

When planners get into the realm of creating rules and regulations for street width, sidewalks, the amount of openings in a wall that fronts on a public street, the planting of street trees, and a host of other design restrictions, it becomes pretty clear that the distinction between the environmental design fields is not clear. The overlap here is with urban designers, landscape architects, architects, transportation engineers, and planners.

Figure 3.6 . . .

The set-back of a house from its property line, the inclusion of a sidewalk and the provision for street trees in the publicly owned right-of-way.

The reality is that city planning departments and private planning consulting firms usually have individuals from each of these backgrounds on their staffs to bring that added perspective to the planners' work.

City planners, through their actions, can mold the very character of a city. In Figure 3.7 we can see the very strict height limitation placed on a majority of the city of Paris. This height limitation maintains the historical character and scale of the city and is very important to Paris being Paris. Equally important is the decision of planners to allow modern high-rise buildings in Paris, but to limit them to a specific district, le Defense. You can see le Defense in the distance on the right hand side of the photograph. This allows Paris to continue to develop within its existing core and to develop the new Paris in its new district. In contrast the city of London has allowed the development of high-rise buildings within its old city. (See Figure 3.8) Here we see tall buildings like the National Westminster Bank and the Swiss Re headquarters adding to the existing skyline of London. The planners have, however, controlled the height of buildings near the river to create a more open and inviting space within the city at the river.

The scope of a planners work is so huge that many planners choose to specialize within planning. Planners may become specialists in housing and housing redevelopment and work to maintain, expand and improve the hous-

Figure 3.7 . . .

Height limitations in Paris with the high-rise district in the distance.

Figure 3.8 . . .

The high-rise section of downtown London.

Figure 3.9...

The proposed development of neighborhoods along the Mississippi River in downtown Minneapolis. The highlighted circular areas designate newly developed neighborhoods adjacent to the river.

ing conditions within their city. They may also become engaged in neighborhood issues and work with grass-roots neighborhood associations to make sure that local groups of people can be heard at city hall and that their desires and dreams for their own neighborhoods are attended to. The neighborhood is one of the most powerful political entities within the city and it is the building block of all great cities. If a city has great neighborhoods, it will be a great city.

Some planners may work within a redevelopment agency to work on the improvement of parts of the city that have been neglected in the past and become eyesores or unhealthy places to live and work. Planners may specialize in recreation or park planning as mentioned above. They may become specialized in transportation issues such as transit planners or pedestrian advocates, or bicycle planners. Some city planners work to provide incentives for people or companies to move into a particular part of the city and improve the economic mix of the city.

The scale or specialization of a planner's work is not the only unique part of their work. Planners, more than any other discipline in environmental design, interact extensively with the public. This is particularly true of planners that work in city planning offices but also applies to planners in private consulting firms. Planners that work for a city planning department typically need to have their work approved, accepted and adopted by a governing body of the city. This governing body may be a planning commission or a city commission.

## THE EDUCATION OF PLANNERS

The planning field is one of two within environmental design that does not require a license from the state in order to practice. Serious planners, however, often pursue certification through an examination process administered by the professional organization of planners within the United States. The American Institute of Certified Planners, a subgroup of the American Planning Association, develops and administers a test that establishes a professional level of knowledge, education and professionalism for those individuals that successfully complete the exam. Eligibility to take the exam is determined by combinations of education and number of years working in the planning field. The easiest way to qualify to take the exam is to have a planning degree from an accredited planning program. There are sixteen schools offering accredited bachelor's degrees in planning and 68 schools offering accredited master's level degrees in planning. There is tremendous value in attracting people with experience in other areas of study such as architecture, landscape architecture, environmental science, geography, political science, etc. to planning in order to bring divergent views and experiences to the field. The number of accredited graduate degree programs compared to the number of undergraduate programs is an indication of the value placed on this diversity of experience and knowledge. The undergraduate programs are typically four years in duration while the graduate programs are one to two years in length. The programs may have a variety of titles such as: urban and environmental planning, city planning, city and regional planning, urban planning and policy, urbanism, environmental policy and planning, and urban and regional planning. Each different title gives a hint to the slant or specialization taught in that particular program. Students should explore the various educational offerings around North America if you are interested in pursuing environmental design at its largest scale: planning.

# Urban Design

Urban design has the least specific definition of its work in all of the environmental design fields. Urban designers are part planner, part architect, and part landscape architect. They are also often part sociologist, part anthropologist, and part politician. People trained in architecture, planning, or landscape architecture who have found that their primary interest lies in the quality and livability of the urban environment often gravitate to urban design. Urban design exists in a vacuum between architecture, landscape architecture, and planning in the urban environment. For many years nobody seemed to be paying attention to the quality of the spaces between buildings and the spaces, activities, and institutions that create a sense of community in our cities. The places of character and uniqueness were disappearing from our cities at the same time that we were building banal suburbs with no character and no sense of community. We seemed to be loosing the things that defined us as communal people.

Many forces have been at work within our society that have contributed to this loss of community and urbanity. The availability of the automobile and inexpensive gasoline literally fueled a flight from the city to an environment that is dominated by the care and feeding of the automobile. Many suburban houses have more space dedicated to the storage of automobiles than they have dedicated to living. The personal mobility offered by the automobile is both astonishing and addicting. We do indeed have a love affair with the car.

*Figure 3.10 . . .*

Houses totally hidden by the spaces dedicated to the automobile. Unfortunately, this is not an uncommon sight for most of our cities in the United States.

The automobile is not the only culprit in the degradation of our civic spaces. In the 1960's our cities were dragged, kicking and screaming, into the "modern" era by reform minded planners and architects. Huge chunks of our cities were torn down and replaced by gleaming new buildings with no relationship to the city or to the region in which they were built. All accomplished under the banner of urban renewal. Most of this work was undertaken by "modernists" who advocated for a new approach to our cities, wiping out the decaying parts of our cities and starting over with a clean slate. Modernism espoused a common architectural language for all of mankind. Unfortunately, the universal architecture of modernism was universally hated by most of the population. We haven't yet recovered from the devastation of urban renewal.

Other social forces have also contributed to our loss of urbanism. Our movement toward more individual forms of entertainment like the television or the iPod divorce us from our surroundings either physically or psychologically. People spend much more time pursuing individual entertainment than ever before. Even when we are walking on the streets we are plugged in to headphones instead of listening and connecting with our surroundings. In addition, much of our public space has been privatized. We no longer meet on the public street as we shop; we meet in the private shopping mall. This limits our ability to connect with each other. Our tendency to treat shopping as our primary social activity means that we can only connect during business hours. In recent years we have heard a great deal of complaining about how disconnected we feel from each other. This, at a time when we are more connected with more people in more parts of the world than ever before. Chatting with people on line from all over the world is easy, talking with our friends can happen anyplace and anytime. And yet we feel more and more isolated. Our connections have become largely virtual. On-line gaming even takes us into virtual worlds so we can team up with virtual people to fight virtual villains in virtual time, with virtual stimulus. Even video-conferences or video telephone calls have an unreal character to them. We learn so much from having a person right next to us as we talk. Body language and gesture are as important to communication as are the words. The subtlety and depth of our communication is lost in our virtual world. We are longing for real connection in real places. This desire has not gone unnoticed by urban designers. Their work is largely driven by our innate need to connect with other people and to make real connections with the environment around us.

Over fifty percent of the world's population now lives in cities. There are many reasons for this including job opportunities or educational opportunities or better social services, but part of the reason is this desire that we have to make connections with other people. We have even begun to see pretty strong flight from the suburbs to the urban centers. It is just more fun in the center. The suburbs are boring. People are seeking urban spaces of high quality; that is the work of the urban designer.

Figure 3.11 . . .

A really bad relationship between the sidewalk and a building. This one is in San Francisco but it can be found in any city.

Urban designers are concerned with how buildings treat the public sidewalk. Do the buildings permit and encourage activity at the street level or do they shut off activity and turn a blank face to the public? They are also concerned with the greening of our urban environment and whether we can generate enough oxygen within the city for the people of the city.[3] Urban designers care about our ability to create community and want to help us feel like we belong to something that is great and that we care about. Urban designers are about opportunity and choice in our urban areas. They are about great gatherings and intimate spaces. They are about celebrations and contemplation. They are about preserving the best of our past and exploring the possibilities of our future. Urban designers are about helping people and nature and our cities to maintain a balanced, exciting, and high quality of life. Urban designers are concerned about how safe you are on the streets and how safe it is to cross the street. They want us all to be healthy and fit and to make sure that we have opportunities to make that the case. Urban designers are about allowance. The ability to allow people to have fun, be safe, work, love, play and connect with their urban environment.

[3]In addition to a concern for the development of oxygen in our cities, we should also be concerned with whether we can take excess carbon (mostly from cars and industry, which causes greenhouse warming of our planet) out of our environment and render it benign.

Figure 3.12 . . .

A public protest held on Justin Herman Plaza in downtown San Francisco.

Figure 3.13 . . .

The Crystal Court in Minneapolis, Minnesota. The "living room" of Minneapolis, designed by Philip Johnson and John Burgee.

Figure 3.14 . . .

A little bit of solitude in downtown Fargo, North Dakota.

Figure 3.15 . . .

A weekend Farmer's Market in downtown Minneapolis. One of those great events that are fun to run across in a downtown.

The list below is adapted from Michael Sorkin's book *Some Assembly Required*.[4] I believe it helps us to simplify some of our responses to the difficult urban design questions posed above. Like most lists it is too simple, the problems are very complex.

- We must **Reinforce Neighborhoods.** Neighborhoods are the building blocks of cities. A neighborhood is an area that people can relate to. It is an area that they feel comfortable within. Neighborhoods are also a great vehicle for communication and governance in the city.

- **Make It Sustainable.** Whatever decisions we make as an urban designer they should contribute to a more sustainable environment for the planet. Each decision should reduce our energy usage, or reduce our material consumption, or reduce the amount of pollution contributed or something else as long as the focus is on sustainability. Whatever the decision, it should be a positive step to a balanced existence with our natural environment.

- One specific way of improving our sustainability is to **Add Green** to our cities. Not only does the creation of more green in our cities provide oxygen and help clean our air and water, it provides opportunities for us to socialize and become active participants in our surroundings.

- Our cities cannot grow indefinitely. One strategy to help deal with sprawling growth is to **Secure the Edge** of our cities. Our survival as a society requires that we protect the sources of our food. Rampant growth of our cities consumes much of the best agricultural land that we have available. If we control the growth of cities we can accomplish two goals: we can protect valuable farm land and we encourage our cities to develop in more efficient and sustainable ways.

- Urban designers must keep in mind the erosion of our public spaces. They must fight against privatizing those spaces that allow us to truly create community. So, urban designers should **Make Public Places.**

- Urban designers don't design buildings but they do, at times, set the standards for the buildings that will be built in our cities. One standard that all urban designers should insist on is that all habitable spaces in buildings have access to **Natural Light and Views to the Outside**. Not only does this decrease energy usage it increases significantly the quality of the space for its users.

- Since the Industrial Revolution planners have segregated the various uses within the city. When dirty or noisy industry is involved this makes a great deal of sense. When compatible uses are involved it does not. The mix of uses in our cities has become so segregated that it is impossible to get from one use to another with using an automobile. We have also built huge tracts of single family homes that create middle class ghettos that empty out during the day and limited our cities to office uses that empty out at night. Neither of these conditions is safe or sustainable. Urban designers must **Finesse the Mix** to create more mixed use and more choices for the citizens of our cities.

- **Reorder Transportation Priorities.** Since World War II our transportation priorities have been to consider the automobile first, followed by transit options and finally when everything else is solved,

[4]Sorkin, Michael. (2001). *Some Assembly Required*. University of Minnesota Press, Minneapolis.

consider the pedestrian. To create more sustainable, healthy, communal cities we must reorder this transportation triumvirate to place the most importance on the pedestrian, secondary importance on the transit system and then, and only then, consider the ease of using the automobile.

- **Localize Architecture and Urban Design.** Urban designers must create the conditions and controls necessary to allow local design standards to create unique spaces linked to our region, our weather, our culture and our history. Seattle, Washington is not like Key West, Florida nor is it like Paris, France nor should it be like either of them. Seattle should be Seattle.

- **Privacy is a concern for everyone.** Around the world privacy is a value that changes considerably with cultural influence. The amount and degree of privacy desired is different in China, Italy and the United States. The density of our urban settings does not have to compromise our individual privacy. Urban designers must **Protect Privacy** in our work but we also must protect it in culturally significant ways.

- **Make It Beautiful.** Beauty is almost lost to us today. It is important. I have included a much longer discussion about the need for beauty in Part 5 of this book.

This list of tasks or priorities is not the final checklist for urban designers. No such thing exists. Like all of the environmental design fields the problems faced by urban design are very complex and interrelated. Successful urban design cannot exist in a vacuum. It relies on successful design work from planners, architects, and landscape architects.

Because the focus of urban design's work is on the public realm, the nature of the design work is different than the work of architects, landscape architects, and interior designers who most often work with individual clients. The client for urban design is the public. Urban designers work within city planning agencies, for large development corporations or for private consulting companies. The people that they impact the most with their work, however, are largely unknown to them. The urban designers know their clients mostly as groups within the community and they often represent these community groups to the city and private corporations. There is a strong advocacy role in urban design involving representation of the little guy, the underdog or the common man.

*Figure 3.16 . . .*

A proposed urban design plan for the Mississippi Riverfront in downtown Minneapolis. One of several proposals by a variety of urban design firms from around the world at the invitation of The Cunningham Group of Minneapolis. Atelier Heamavihio created this proposal.

*Figure 3.17 . . .*

An accompanying sketch of a proposed light-rail transit line as part of the above urban design proposal.

## COMMUNITY DESIGN

In the decades of the 1960's and 1970's the climate of protest over our participation in the Viet Nam conflict extended into many other facets of life. People became very involved in social justice causes including issues pertaining to urban design. In a number of cities in the United States community design centers were founded by architects, planners, and urban designers that wanted to improve the quality of life for everyone in the city, particularly the downtrodden. These community design centers became advocates for low income housing, for preservation and for the rights of citizen groups. The community design movement was often associated with design schools at a local university but many centers were established as private non-profit corporations. The driving force behind these centers was to serve people in their quest for a better life. It was very difficult for community design centers to keep their doors open. They served mostly poor clients that could not pay very much in fees, so the designers supplemented fees with grants from the federal government or local governments. It was a very difficult way to make a living for those designers dedicated enough to work in the centers. Many of the centers around the country closed down in the late 70's and 80's. They did excellent work and helped thousands of people, but it became extremely difficult to make enough money to pay the environmental designers that chose to help society through the community design centers.

It has been 40 years since the beginning of the community design movement and environmental design has rediscovered its heart. The small number of community design centers that survived from the 60's have become stronger and more adept at serving their communities. In addition, many new centers are being established to serve people of need throughout the country, both rural and urban. The projects being completed by today's community design centers include the design and construction of low-income housing, job training, educational support in urban areas, repair of existing housing stock to keep it from deteriorating and to keep elderly owners from losing their independence, converting parking lots into functioning wet lands, helping communities improve their urban design, helping neighborhood groups to organize and improve their living conditions, making homes handicapped accessible, and representing the underdog in development situations. The service opportunities available through the community design centers are important for all environmental designers. They keep us in touch with many of the nitty gritty issues that we face in our cities, and provide invaluable services for thousands of people that could not otherwise afford them.

*Figure 3.18 . . .*

The main shopping street in Liverpool, England on a typical weekday at noon. The use of public space in Europe is very different from the use of public space in the United States. European cultures place a higher value on public participation than do Americans.

## INVOLVING THE PUBLIC

In much the same way that planners engage the public in their design work, urban designers find that their work requires the involvement of the people that will be living and working in their designs. Urban designers need to find out what people want, specifically, in their urban surroundings. This is particularly important when we consider the goal to make each urban center a reflection of the region it is in and the culture that lives there.

Urban design often involves the dreams and aspirations of a neighborhood or of the whole city. How does one determine what those dreams are unless the people get involved in the process? Urban designers have developed a number of strategies to get the public involved in helping to create their own future. Urban design projects will often involve large, open invitation, public meetings where ideas are shared, options evaluated or opinions expressed. These meetings are effective at getting and understanding information but they are not particularly effective at getting the

Figure 3.19...

Cultural difference within cities is equally important. This photograph is from China Town in San Francisco during the Chinese New Year in 2006. The space, the look, the smells, the activities are different in China Town than in other parts of the city.

Figure 3.20...

An action photograph from a design charrette conducted in Grand Forks, North Dakota in 1997. Grand Forks had just suffered a catastrophic flood and fire that devastated their downtown area. Atelier Heamavihio of Fargo, North Dakota conducted the charrette.

Figure 3.21...

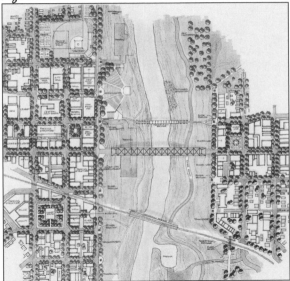

The plan for renewal of downtown Grand Forks, North Dakota and East Grand Forks, Minnesota that was the result of the charrette shown above.

public behind the direction of the work. A design charrette has become the preferred method of engaging the public in ideas and decisions that impact their future.

In a charrette, participants from the city are engaged, along with the design professionals, in design exercises that help determine the future direction of their city or neighborhood. The charrette process takes a considerable amount of time to prepare and it takes some time commitment on the part of the participants, often two or three days to complete the work. The urban design consultant will take the results from the charrette and develop them further and refine them to create a final urban design strategy. That final strategy will again be presented to the public for their comments and approval.

Many firms that do urban design work utilize the charrette process. The firm of DPZ (Duany, Plater-Zyberk and Company) from Miami, Florida is well known for their creation of new communities using the charrette process. They engage the public in the overall design of the community and in the development of the urban codes and regulations as well.

## EDUCATING URBAN DESIGNERS

Urban design does not have a process for licensing individuals that practice in the field. In fact, most people that are involved in urban design have been trained, at least initially, in another one of the environmental design fields. It is very common for a person that was trained in landscape architecture, planning or architecture to find a real interest in the urban condition and seek to pursue work within urban design. There are educational opportunities for degrees in urban design and most of them are graduate degrees offered through design programs. Most of the urban design programs are post-professional design degree programs that last two or three semesters. As post-professional programs they typically require the incoming students to have completed a professional degree in architecture, planning, landscape architecture or interior design. The degree titles are typically something like Masters in Urban Design or Master of Architecture in Urban Design.

Although urban design is the newcomer to the environmental design fields, it fills a much needed void and is a field with a tremendous need for practitioners.

# Landscape Architecture

*Chapter 8*

Landscape architecture, as a recognized profession, is a relatively young member of the environmental design fields. According to historians the term "landscape architect" was first used by author John Claudius Loudon in the title of a book about the work of Humphrey Repton in 1841. Although not broadly used, the term came up several times in the writings of Frederick Law Olmsted as he discussed the roles that he and architect Calvert Vaux took in the competition to design New York City's Central Park. Shortly after Olmsted and Vaux won the competition for Central Park—their entry was called Greensward—Frederick Law Olmsted was named the superintendent of the park and shortly after that the "architect-in-chief" of the park. Olmsted was uncomfortable using the term "architect" since his partner Calvert Vaux was an architect and one of the founding members of the American Institute of Architects. Olmsted preferred the term "landscape artist" but landscape architect seemed to stick. To this day environmental designers engaged in the creation of large, or small landscape spaces are landscape architects. To legally use the term "landscape architect" you must have completed all of the requirements for licensure and passed the licensing exam.

Even though the term landscape architect is fairly recent, the work of landscape architecture has been around for quite a while. The specialized work of the landscape architect grew out of the tradition of the master gardener in the 17th century. The work of gardeners had been getting more and more complex over the previous two hundred years. People of wealth were interested in creating stunning private outdoor spaces for their enjoyment: spaces that were protected from the mass of humanity around them. These gardens become bigger and bigger and so elaborate that the gardener was required to step away from the gardening itself and become a designer of the garden, the "master gardener."

Figure 3.22 . . .

The main axis of the Gardens at Versailles by Le Nôtre. The tightly controlled vistas, plantings, gardens, pools, and sculpture are hallmarks of the "French style" of landscape architecture.

Figure 3.23 . . .

The main axis of the Gardens at Versailles after the trees had been trimmed as they had been in Louis XIV's time. The gardens are undergoing major renovation to return them back to their previous splendor.

*Figure 3.24 . . .*

The garden views to the south from the Chateau at Versailles. Landscape Architect—Le Nôtre.

*Figure 3.25 . . .*

The Lower Parterre of the Orangery designed by Le Nôtre. The gardens are surrounded on three sides by buildings designed by Jardoin-Mansart that house and protect the citrus trees during France's cold winters.

*Figure 3.26 . . .*

The three tier fountains being renovated in the summer of 2004. Workers are tying hundreds of sea shells onto the fountains as part of the finishing touches of their restoration.

Frenchman Le Nôtre was just such a "master gardener." He worked on the design of the Jardins de Versailles for Louis XIV from about 1661 until 1687. The gardens are immense and represented the grandeur of the French culture to thousands of visitors to the seat of Louis XIV's government. Louis loved these gardens so much that from 1689 to 1705 he wrote six different guides to viewing the gardens. He set out paths and descriptions of the various parts of the gardens so that his guests could enjoy the gardens as much as he did.[5]

The Gardens at Versailles are immense and are therefore very costly to maintain. The gardens and chateau have long ago passed into the hands of the French government and have been converted into a living museum of French culture. What was built as a private enclave has become a public space for French citizens and a tourist destination for visitors. Unfortunately, the gardens have become very overgrown and dilapidated. They were still very impressive, but would have been totally unrecognizable to Louis XIV or Le Nôtre. In the 1990's the French government made a major commitment to restore the gardens to the height of their development when Louis was king. This was a tremendous undertaking, but it is indicative of the stewardship nature of landscape architects worldwide. A hallmark of landscape architecture is the strong commitment to be stewards of the environment whether that environment is natural or man-made.

Landscape architecture is unique in that landscape architects create living environments that change remarkably as they age and grow. This means that landscape architects must create environments that look good and work well the day they are completed, and that look good and work well many years later as the landscape grows and matures. It takes a great deal of knowledge and a keen imagination to be able to accurately envision a landscape project 25 years after you have created it. The Gardens at Versailles are an extreme example of a landscape that is mostly left to its own devises. The decision to renovate the gardens was a great decision but the consequences are staggering. If you visit the gardens now you will find areas of the gardens totally devoid of vegetation. You will also find fountains and sculpture in various states of repair and restoration. But, you will also find areas that are beginning to grow back and show the remarkable nature of this grand garden. It will be truly

[5]Louis XIV. (1992, 1689). *The Way to Present the Gardens of Versailles.* Réunion des Musées nationaux, Paris.

Figure 3.27 . . .

The Hamlet at Versailles. This garden within the garden
was created for Marie Antoinette.

Figure 3.28 . . .

Green Park in London. This park is a great example of
the English picturesque landscape style. Although the park
looks very natural it is a completely created landscape.

incredible in a few years, but I would encourage anyone to visit now to see how an historic landscape needs care and rejuvenation just like an historic building does or an historic section of a city.

Most of the Gardens at Versailles are in the formal French tradition but one section was developed in the picturesque "English Garden" tradition. This section of the garden, called The Hamlet, was created for Marie Antoinette, Louis' wife.

The English landscape architects preferred to create more naturalistic, picturesque landscapes. Even when starting from scratch, like was done at Green Park in London, the landscape architects created a design that looked like it had been there for all time. The difference between the formal French landscape tradition and the naturalistic English landscape tradition is still with us today. We still see examples of formal landscapes today and informal landscapes. The formal tradition is still being carried on in France as seen in the very formal design for the Parc André Citroen in Paris by Gilles Clement and Alain Provost and the abstract, but formal work of Martha Schwartz in the United States.

The English tradition lives on in practically every city in the United States. Most city parks are designed in the tradition of Frederick Law Olmstead's Central Park. Natural looking bodies of water with groves of trees and wandering paths create restful and picturesque spaces for the hectic life in the United States. Frederick Law Olmsted believed that landscape design was not just a technical or artistic endeavor but was a social and civic responsibility. Talking about Central Park, Olmsted said:

Figure 3.29 . . .

Parc André Citroen in Paris by Gilles Clement and Alain Provost. The City of Paris sponsored a competition to design this park on an abandoned automobile factory site. The competition jury could not decide between Clement and Provost so they asked them to combine their solutions into one proposal for the park. Both landscape architects created formal relationships between plantings, buildings, and the paths for movement throughout the park and their different solutions combine quite interestingly in this new formal park. Shown is part of the north side designed by Gilles Clement.

## Figure 3.30 . . .

The south side of Parc André Citroen, designed by Alain Provost.

## Figure 3.31 . . .

The plaza in front of the Federal Building in downtown Minneapolis by landscape architect Martha Schwartz. This formal placement of abstracted glacial deposits creates an interesting, inviting and protective frontispiece to the Federal Building.

## Figure 3.32 . . .

A view in New York's Central Park by landscape architect's Olmsted and Vaux.

*It is one great purpose of the Park to supply to the hundreds of thousands of tired workers, who have no opportunity to spend their summers in the country, a specimen of God's handiwork that shall be to them, inexpensively, what a month or two in the White Mountains or the Adirondacks is, at great cost, to those in easier circumstances.*[6]

Landscape architecture's tradition may come from the grand gardens of Europe but the modern day landscape architect creates a much broader set of landscapes in their drive to be stewards of the environment. Landscape architects may be involved in projects that range in scope from a backyard vegetable garden for a wheelchair bound client, to a huge regional biking and hiking system of trails and activities. Their work has expanded to include such technically complex landscapes as "healing landscapes" associated with hospitals, restorative landscapes that provide oxygen for a building and clean the air of that building, to a natural sewage treatment system where vegetation processes human waste resulting in clean water that is put back into the natural environment in a constructed wetland. They have also been called upon to increase security for buildings. The plaza in front of the Federal Building in Minneapolis is a good example. Martha Schwartz created a landscape that is inviting but that also makes it almost impossible for someone to drive a vehicle into the main floor of the building. Landscape architects are still involved in creating private gardens for wealthy clients but more commonly they are providing services for communities and corporations as well as individuals. Landscape architects are critical for the sustainable design of new communities. They provide the most direct link between our built environment and the natural environment. Balance between the two is a critical issue for landscape architects. As an example, most of our strategies for removing excess carbon from our atmosphere (the part of greenhouse gases that cause global warming) involve the creation of landscapes that convert carbon into more useful compounds.

[6]Rybczynski, Witold. (1999). *A Clearing in the Distance: Frederick Law Olmsted and America in the Nineteenth Century*. Scribner, New York. Page 177.

Landscape architects deal with the broadest scope of work of any of the environmental design fields. The work is very technical and also very artistic. In recent years the knowledge base for landscape architecture has increased dramatically with the emphasis being placed on sustainability. Plants and their properties have always been important to landscape architects, but now they need to know much more about the chemical processes that the plants utilize to know how to use them in sustainable situations. In order to help understand the complexities of the field, Patrick Condon has proposed a landscape typology within which landscapes and their characteristics can be classified.[7] His system moves from the most natural landscape spaces to the most humanly controlled and then back to the natural while tracing from the most simple to the most complex. This is a very interesting way to look at the landscape around us and to introduce some important words into our design vocabulary.

- Natural Clearing
- Single Tree
- Clearing
- Cloister—a tranquil green space surrounded by a covered arcade as in a monastic center.
- Square—a town square
- Street
- Front Yard
- Back Yard
- Allee—trees planted in a single line
- Orchard
- Bosque—trees planted on a regular grid but not fruit trees
- Natural Forest

*Figure 3.33 . . .*

A beautiful alee at Greenwood Terrace in Berkeley, California designed by landscape architect Lawrence Halprin.

These elements become the building blocks for landscape architects. They also help us understand the relationships between natural landscapes that are able to heal themselves and maintain their essential ecological balance, and the human landscapes that must be carefully monitored and controlled to keep from overtaxing the natural systems. The goal for most landscape architects is to create beautiful spaces while ensuring that we can maintain the ecological health of the planet. As a further illustration of this duality, Professor Condon presents the list above as a "reasoned" approach to landscape architecture where the realm of reason is about thinking, ordering, computing and concluding. He contrasts the presentation of this list with an "imaginative" presentation of the same information. The realm of the "imaginative" deals with sensations, visions,

*Figure 3.34 . . .*

A bosque of young trees on the campus of the University of Utah in Salt Lake City.

[7]Condon, Patrick. *A Built Landscape Typology: The Language of the Land We Live In.* Published in Frank, Karen A. & Lynda H. Schneekloth, eds. (1994) *Ordering Space: Types in Architecture and Design.* Can Nostrand Reinhold, New York.

pleasure, pain, stimulation and need.[8] Landscape architecture, like all of the environmental design fields relies on science and logic as well as art and emotion to create our landscapes.

## LANDSCAPE ARCHITECTURE FIRMS

Most landscape architecture firms are small consulting firms from one to twenty-five people. They may be organized as a private company with only one owner, be a partnership with multiple owners or be a corporation with several stockholders. One form of ownership does not provide any particular advantage over another. Some landscape architecture firms are very large and might employ several hundred employees. Landscape architecture firms, like most other consulting environmental design firms do not limit their work to landscape architecture. They will very typically include planning and urban design services, and may include engineering or construction services as well.

Besides working in a consulting firm, many landscape architects find themselves working in city planning offices, city parks departments, with real estate developers or for multi-discipline design firms that offer services in all of the environmental design fields. The largest single employer of landscape architects in the United States is the federal government. Hundreds of landscape architects work for the National Park Service or the Forest Service to design and protect the thousands of acres held in the public trust for our use. The work of these dedicated landscape architects makes a substantial contribution to a national system of public space that is the envy of the world.

## EDUCATION OF LANDSCAPE ARCHITECTS

In order to practice landscape architecture as a profession you would need both an education from an accredited landscape architecture program and a license from the state. Landscape architecture is licensed in each state in the United States and in most countries around the globe. In the United States the Council of Landscape Architecture Registration Boards (CLARB) has developed a common licensing exam that is administered throughout the country. A prerequisite for taking the licensing exam is a professional landscape architecture degree from an accredited program. A professional degree in landscape architecture is usually a five-year bachelor of landscape architecture degree but might also be a master's degree in landscape architecture. The most important aspect of picking a landscape architecture program is that it be accredited by the Landscape Architecture Accrediting Board (LAAB), otherwise any degree obtained from that institution will not apply toward licensure.

[8]Ibid. Page 79.

# Architecture

On the surface, architecture may seem to be the most easily defined of the environmental design fields. Architecture is about buildings; the design, engineering and construction of buildings. So what is so hard to understand about that? The influence of a building's design on its environment is not limited to the exterior wall of the building. Buildings relate to each other, they create urban spaces, they define landscape spaces, and they are filled with interior spaces. The lines of definition that separate the environmental design fields are indeed blurry. Architecture is "the art or science of building; specifically the art or practice of designing and building structures and especially habitable ones."[9] For many people that are in architecture, the combination of art and science that is pointed out in the definition is a very important aspect of the field. Architecture combines the technology and knowledge base of the sciences with the sensibility, grace and creativity of art. As discussed before, we use the term "design" to convey this combination of art and science. It is applicable to all of the environmental design fields. The second part of the definition of architecture deals with the building of structures that are occupied by people, habitation. Although architecture is primarily focused on providing habitation for people there are some architects that have been involved in providing habitation for other types of life forms. I worked on the design of a prairie dog town many years ago for the Hogle Zoological Gardens in Salt Lake City. The habitation needs of prairie dogs are very different than the needs of people. Additionally, a new and growing segment of architecture is the creation of virtual buildings and environments. These virtual buildings are not inhabited by the usual cast of characters, but instead create the environment in which computer games are played. Virtual architects are also creating the cities and buildings in which many of our major motion pictures are set.

Architects are regulated in their practice by the governments of most countries around the world. In the United States, each individual state separately licenses architects which gives them the right to practice within that state. Each state places the responsibility for its citizens' health, safety, and welfare on the architect as it relates to the buildings they create. This responsibility includes the structural integrity of the building as well as its safe functioning day to day. It also includes making buildings accessible to all people regardless of their physical or mental capabilities and the protection of people in the event of emergencies requiring evacuation. Most of these responsibilities are included in the building codes adopted by each jurisdiction. Over the years many different building codes have been written and enforced. Luckily for all environmental designers the building code groups have gotten together and combined many of the most utilized codes into the *International Building Code* which is now being adopted in most states and in most countries around the world. This makes the job of architects and other environmental designers a bit easier when the rules are consistent in this age of global commerce.

[9]Merriam-Webster, Inc. *Merriam-Webster's Collegiate Dictionary, Tenth Edition.* (1993). Merriam-Webster, Incorporated. Springfield, MA. Page 61.

Early in human history, construction became complex enough that specialized knowledge was required to design the important buildings. Architects today require a tremendous amount of knowledge about people, technology, materials, construction, safety, health, and the environment in order to perform their duties. Years ago, in a more simple time, architects were capable of completing all design aspects of a building project. Today the economics and complexity of our work makes it almost impossible for an individual architect to complete a project alone. Architects work in teams. They assemble around them specialist architects in the areas they need, as well as engineers, interior designers, material specialists, code specialists, fire protection specialists, elevator specialists, etc. to create teams of people to design today's multi-use

Figure 3.35 . . .

The amphitheater in Millennium Park by Frank Gehry.

buildings. The long held image of the architect as a lone wolf, working by *himself*, against tremendous odds to bring his great creation into being is just not true any more. Even our current "hero architects" like Frank Gehry, cannot create their buildings by themselves. Gehry is the architect out front with the media and he is the creative genius behind the work, but he has a huge team of architects, engineers and artists working to make it possible to build his buildings. Howard Roark, Ann Rand's quintessential architect in *The Fountainhead*, just is not possible today. His idealism is still important, his isolation is not.

The traditional image of an architect is that they are always men. I cannot think of a film that has a woman architect as the main character. In fact, I cannot even think of an instance when an architect in a film is portrayed by a woman. Architecture has been a male dominated profession for much of its history. Like the other major professions of medicine and law, architecture is now a mixed gender profession. Enrollment in architecture schools around the United States is typically 50% female. Graduation rates are approaching 50% female. And, women are making their way into the top positions in architectural firms worldwide. Women are not yet represented in enough of the ownership positions but they are moving up through the ranks. The architectural firms are changing rapidly but engineering and the construction trades have been much slower to welcome women into their midst. Twenty years ago it was very unusual to find a woman on a construction site. Today it is much more common to find women in the construction trades as well as in all of the environmental design fields. Architecture has benefited tremendously from the influence of women in the field. It is just not possible to do excellent work when half of the society is not represented in the creative processes involved in building our environment.

The other tradition in architecture is that its practitioners have not only been male but white. This stereotype is not really correct today but it is too correct. Cultural diversity within architecture is changing just as it is in many fields of endeavor but it is not changing quickly enough. Again, in order to do excellent work we must have the experiences, expertise and background of a wide range of people. Minority groups are not yet represented in the environmental design fields in numbers matching their population. This is a challenge for architecture as well as all of the other environmental design fields. I live and teach in a part of the United States that has a relatively high representation of Native Americans. For a host of reasons that we don't really understand or even glimpse, the numbers of Native Americans pursuing degrees in environmental design is staggeringly low. We have, it seems, at most one Native American in our programs at a time. Both the Native American community and the environmental design fields are suffering because of this. This is a great challenge and an opportunity for change.

# RESIDENTIAL ARCHITECTURE

Many students come to universities throughout the United States to study architecture believing that architects mostly design single family houses. Although there are architects that specialize in single family residences, and do an incredible job with their design, a vast majority of the single family housing in the United States has never been touched by an architect. Although architects are charged with maintaining the health, safety and welfare of the public, related to the buildings that we use, a quirk in the licensing laws exempts single family homes from this charge. Pressure from the home builders of this country continue to be felt by public licensing agencies; pressure to not only exempt single family homes but much larger housing projects as well. It is self-serving of me to say that I believe all buildings should be designed by architects, but I do believe that ALL BUILDINGS SHOULD BE DESIGNED BY ARCHITECTS. Our increasing understanding of the impact that buildings have on the sustainability of our environment makes it vitally important that every building be designed and constructed in ways that do not over tax our environmental systems but return value and substance to those systems. I believe strongly that every shed designed and built should comply with this mandate.

The types of buildings that an architect might design are very broad but can be classified in four different realms of practice. The four realms of practice are: residential, commercial, institutional and industrial.

Even though most single family homes built in the world do not have the benefit of an architect's expertise, residential projects can be a substantial part of many architecture practices. A single family home is an essential building for architects. It is a building in which the desires of the clients are most directly felt and accommodated. Many architects undertake single family homes as an important part of their practice. Several architects over the years, such as Frank Gehry, have used their own homes as design experiments to explore new expressions, new technologies, and new ways of living.

The larger percentage of the residential work completed by architects is in multiple family residential buildings. These projects may involve condominium developments, apartment buildings, low-income housing undertaken for a city, or high-rise residential towers in urban centers.

*Figure 3.36 . . .*

Architect Bruce Hella's home in Fargo, North Dakota.

*Figure 3.37 . . .*

The Robie House in Chicago by Frank Lloyd Wright.

Figure 3.38 . . .

A condominium building at the Snowbird Ski Resort, Alta, Utah by Brixen and Christopher Architects.

Figure 3.39 . . .

Town homes in Maple Grove, Minnesota.

Figure 3.40 . . .

Subsidized rental housing in San Francisco.

Figure 3.41 . . .

The St. Regis tower in San Francisco by Skidmore, Owings, and Merrill Architects. This is a mixed-use tower with a hotel at the bottom and condominiums in the top half of the building.

Figure 3.42 . . .

Old mill buildings in Minneapolis that have been renovated into up-scale condominiums. This area of Minneapolis languished for years but has now become the hot place to live.

As the world's population becomes more and more urban, the need for urban forms of housing increases. This is a continuing area of growth for architects, and an opportunity to impact both the city and its sustainability in substantial ways. Many cities are seeing increased demand for downtown housing as well as the more typical suburban single family housing. Architects are rising to the challenge to produce urban housing through a combination of historic renovation, re-use/conversion, and new construction. This work requires close coordination between various environmental designers. The design of suburban housing is an area of architecture that requires a good deal more attention. Suburban sprawl is one contributor to global warming that could and should be addressed by teams of environmental designers.

# COMMERCIAL ARCHITECTURE

A large percentage of architectural work can be classified as commercial work. Commercial buildings are quite simply retail stores and office buildings. Take a look around today and see just how much of our world falls into those two simple categories. Everything from the penny candy store (which I realize is a thing of the past) to the giant office skyscraper falls into commercial architecture. As the projects become more and more complex an architectural firm might specialize in a particular type of building. Some firms may maintain much of their practice by designing high-rise office towers all over the world like the firm of Skidmore, Owings, and Merrill. Tall buildings require very specialized knowledge and experiences on the part of the architect and the other members of the design team. Three of the four photos below are all major office developments designed by Skidmore, Owings, and Merrill. The newest group of tall super skyscrapers is now being designed and built in the Middle East and in the Far East. Architects from all over the world are creating these new towers and new cities.

Offices, of course, are not always high-rise buildings. A majority of office buildings are smaller buildings in a variety of settings, some on large sites away from cities and some within our cities. The two examples on page 70

Figure 3.43 . . .

John Hancock Tower in Chicago,
SOM Architects.

Figure 3.44 . . .

Sears Tower in Chicago, SOM
Architects.

Figure 3.46 . . .

The Swiss Re headquarters tower in
London by Sir Norman Foster. A
highly sustainable high-rise building.
Lloyd's of London by Piano and
Rogers is in the foreground.

Figure 3.45 . . .

The Exchange Building at
Broadgate in London, SOM
Architects.

The Canal + building in Paris by Richard Meier. This building houses the offices and studios of the French television giant. Meier is an architect that continues to practice in the "modernist" tradition.

Figure 3.48...

The Casting Center at Walt Disney World by Robert A. M. Stern. This is an example of an office building in a landscape setting as well as an example of "post-modern style."

give us recent examples of each. We are used to seeing buildings that become a part of the milieu, our background, but not all buildings need to be background. In fact, even background buildings need to be inviting, exciting and pleasant to occupy if we are doing our jobs correctly.

Other firms may develop a particular expertise in very large retail structures like the Mall of America in Bloomington, Minnesota or Horton Plaza in San Diego, California. Over the past two decades our society has shifted its primary public activity to shopping. Shopping is now the number one social activity in the United States and potentially in the world.

This shift has forced architects to create shopping centers that are a party. They are the place that we go to meet other people, to see and be seen. This is not a particularly healthy social condition, but it is the driving force in retail architecture. Active spaces, full of people, color, and smells are a really good thing and many of these shopping areas are fun spaces to be in. Horton Plaza is such a place. At a time when almost everybody was building enclosed downtown shopping malls, the developers and architects in San Diego chose to create a space

Figure 3.49...

Horton Plaza, San Diego, California by the Jerde Partnership.

Figure 3.50...

Horton Plaza, San Diego, California.

Figure 3.51...

Horton Plaza, San Diego, California.

more fitting to the beautiful weather of San Diego. Jon Jerde of the Jerde Partnership designed Horton Plaza in 1985 for the Hahn Company, one of the country's largest shopping center developers. It is fun to be there and it has remained active since it was constructed. The challenge for architects is to create authentic spaces that are visually and culturally linked to the specific region of the country or region of the world in which they are built. It is particularly upsetting to go into a shopping center in Glasgow, Scotland and not be able to tell whether you are in Glasgow or Los Angeles.

Some really great architecture is created in retail developments. Unfortunately, there is an overabundance of poorly designed retail architecture littering our cities. One has only to go to the local shopping mall and look at all of the development around it. Building after building of same-o, same-o. Bad fast food restaurants, bad chain stores, and bad strip retail centers trying to entice us into their banal spaces. The gauntlet has been thrown down. We are being challenged to create better, more engaging and more sustainable retail environments that serve our cities, our shoppers, and our retailers.

## INSTITUTIONAL ARCHITECTURE

Many architectural firms rely on institutional buildings for the bulk of their business. Buildings such as schools, university buildings, hospitals, churches, museums, and civic buildings are considered institutional buildings. They are the buildings and environments that are constructed for public use by the institutions of our society. Institutional architecture is very appealing for firms because it tends to be a steady source of work regardless of the ups and downs of the economy. Institutional work is often the vehicle through which architects can explore new and different solutions and artistic expressions. The range of possibilities seems to be much broader in institutional work. Shown below are a few examples of a variety of institutional buildings that illustrate the individual possibilities for the architect's creative exploration.

*Figure 3.52 . . .*

The de Young museum in San Francisco, California by Herzog and deMuron Architects.

*Figure 3.53 . . .*

The East Gallery of the National Gallery of Art in Washington, D.C. by I. M. Pei Architects.

*Figure 3.54 . . .*

The Weisman Art Museum at the University of Minnesota in Minneapolis by Frank Gehry and Associates.

Figure 3.55 . . .

The Harold Washington Library in Chicago by Hammond, Bebee and Babka Architects.

Figure 3.56 . . .

The Minneapolis Public Library by Cesar Pelli of Pelli Clarke Pelli.

Figure 3.57 . . .

The Bell Tower at the Annunciation Priory and Church in Bismarck, North Dakota by Marcel Breuer.

Figure 3.58 . . .

Gethsemane Episcopal Cathedral in Fargo, North Dakota by Charles Moore of Moore/Andersen Architects.

Figure 3.59 . . .

The new London City Hall by Sir Norman Foster.

Figure 3.60 . . .

A biological research facility at Stanford University by Sir Norman Foster.

The buildings shown previously have been completed since the late 1950's and most within the last twenty years. The oldest, the Annunciation Priory by Marcel Breuer was built between 1954 and 1963. Its soaring bell tower is still a marvel and a bold design statement on the bluffs of the Missouri River. The design of projects like the Harold Washington Library by Hammond, Bebee and Babka and the Gethsemane Cathedral by Moore/Andersen Architects explore historical and cultural symbolism, while the architects of the museum projects explore bold new forms and space making. Although great architecture is being done in all facets of the field, it seems like there is more acceptance for bold ideas within institutional architecture.

*Figure 3.61 . . .*

The Guthrie Theater in Minneapolis by Jean Nouvel.

## INDUSTRIAL ARCHITECTURE

The design of industrial buildings is a small but important part of our built environment. Throughout history a great deal of the buildings constructed for industry have been designed not by architects but by individuals with expertise in the particular process of the industry. As these processes have become more complex and cleaner, and we have begun to understand more clearly the needs of our workers, the design of industrial buildings has become a larger market for architects. Not only can industrial buildings fit the needs of their industry, but they can also contribute to a quality environment through the hard work of teams of dedicated environmental designers.

## SPECIALTY ARCHITECTURAL PRACTICES

Because some buildings are so complex to design and construct, some architectural firms have chosen to specialize in particular niche markets. Some large architectural firms have created separate specialty firms within their

*Figure 3.62 . . .*

The power plant at North Dakota State University designed by Lightowler Johnson Architects and Engineers.

*Figure 3.63 . . .*

A flood water pumping station on the Isle of Dogs, London by John Outram and Associates, Architects.

Figure 3.64...

Camden Yard, home of the Baltimore Orioles.
Designed by HOK Sport.

larger firm to focus on these opportunities. These specialty markets include such buildings as athletic fields, hospitals, historic restoration, hospitality, museums, concert halls, and research laboratory buildings.

HOK (Hellmuth, Obata, and Kassabaum) Sport has designed many of the professional sports facilities in the country including Camden Yard in Baltimore for the Orioles, AT&T Park for the San Francisco Giants, PNC Park for the Pittsburgh Pirates, Gillette Stadium for the New England Patriots, M&T Stadium for the Baltimore Ravens and Telstra Stadium for the Sydney Olympics. This is just a fraction of the athletic facilities that HOK Sport has designed in the last couple of decades. FLAD and Associates Architects are known for designing some of the best research laboratories in the world. They have designed research laboratories for many universities and for private research firms such as the Johnson & Johnson, Eli Lilly, Bayer Corporation, Genentech and Backweston Labs. These facilities are located all over the world. FLAD has offices around the globe, but they are headquartered in Madison, Wisconsin. HOK is headquartered in St. Louis, Missouri. You don't have to be located in a world capital to provide architectural services to the world. Frank Gehry Architects' practice is quite varied. He has done a very large number of world renowned museums including the Guggenheim Museum, Bilbao and the Wiseman Museum in Minneapolis. The firm of Wimberly, Allison, Tong and Goo, headquartered in Los Angeles is perhaps the best known hospitality specialist in the world. They have designed resort hotels all over the world including facilities in Bali, Indonesia; Amman, Jordan; Dubai, United Arab Emirates; Tokyo, Las Vegas and the Bahamas. Each of these firms has developed a particular expertise in a limited but important niche within architectural practice. They have been very successful.

## ARCHITECTURAL FIRM ORGANIZATION

Most architectural firms do work in multiple realms of practice. Most firms do not specialize like those mentioned above. Even HOK does not specialize as an entire firm although they do have two specialty groups, one for sports facilities and one for medical facilities. Architecture firms will do a wide variety of projects and will typically have multiple, differing projects underway at any given time.

A majority of architectural firms are small firms with from one to a dozen people working in them. These firms usually undertake a variety of work and assemble teams of consultants to help them accomplish the solutions that they desire. These small firms are the backbone of the architectural profession. They provide services to small towns and large cities alike.

In order to be an owner in an architecture firm, in most jurisdictions, you must be a licensed architect. This, in addition to the charge to protect the health, safety, and welfare of the public, places a great deal of importance on the schooling and licensing of architects.

# ARCHITECTURE AND A SUSTAINABLE ENVIRONMENT

Chapter 2 in this book looks at the importance of sustainable design across the environmental design fields. It sets the challenges for all of us. The specific responsibility assumed by architects is a substantial part of the sustainability movement. Buildings account for a large percentage of the energy expended around the world, and it is in the architects purview to limit energy usage and material consumption in the buildings they design. As an example, buildings (and therefore architects) are responsible for:

- one-third of the world's total energy use,

- one-half of the total energy use in the United States,

- two-thirds of the nation's electricity use,

- one-fifth of the world's fresh water use,

- the generation of one-half of the nation's solid waste,

- consumption of one-third of the nation's wood, and

- consumption of one-third of all material resources.[10]

Technology is not the only answer to these problems. It helps, but it is not the answer. Serious changes in the way we design, build and use buildings is required. Demands to provide for sustainable design are becoming the norm in architecture. It is not only essential for the continuation of our society and this planet, but it makes good economic sense. The United States Green Building Council has developed a series of programs to help building owners and designers build more sustainable projects. The program is called LEED—Leadership in Energy and Environmental Design. There are different LEED programs set up for new construction, existing buildings, housing and neighborhoods. Each program involves a checklist of the best practices in sustainable design that you can utilize in your buildings. You receive points for each item used, and by accumulating a large enough number of points you can qualify for LEED certification. The certification varies from the lowest level, certified through silver, gold and finally platinum certification. There are very few buildings in the world that currently qualify for platinum LEED certification.

LEED is a really good starting point on our way to a sustainable future for environmental design, but it is not the final answer. Many of the goals being talked about now involve buildings being contributors to the power grid by generating more power than they use and having them consume more carbon than they produce, provide oxygen for all of their inhabitants and so on. The goals are laudable and not just dreams—they are a necessity. The tasks of sustainable design will be the driving force in architecture for the foreseeable future.

[10]Kevin Flynn in a lecture given to the Department of Architecture and Landscape Architecture at North Dakota State University in the fall semester of 2006. Kevin is the president of EcoDEEP, an architectural firm in Minneapolis, Minnesota specializing in sustainable design.

# ARCHITECTURAL EDUCATION

To practice architecture you need to be licensed by the jurisdiction in which you are doing work. That licensure is by individual states in the United States. To qualify to take the exam you must have a professional degree from an accredited educational program and you must complete the Intern Development Program. The Intern Development Program (IDP) consists of a series of required experiences spaced over a three year minimum internship time. This is a paid internship in which you are required to work for a licensed architect.

The degree you are required to have is a professional degree in architecture from a university program accredited by the National Architectural Accreditation Board. The degree designation can vary from university to university and might be a five year Bachelor of Architecture degree or a five year Master of Architecture degree or a six year Master of Architecture degree. Each of these degrees can be accredited as the professional degree for licensure. If you are interested in being licensed as an architect you must attend an accredited university program. All architecture programs are not the same. They differ in emphasis and approach but all must meet the same accreditation requirements. Shop around for a program that fits your individual needs.

# Chapter 10

## Interior Design

Interior design is the youngest of the environmental design fields. This is true only because it is the last of the fields to be independently organized. People have been paying attention to the function and quality of their interior spaces since we first moved a rock in our caves.

Many, if not most, of our memories about a place are wrapped up in our memory of interiors. The color and texture of walls, floors, and materials; the quality of the light bouncing around the space; the smells emanating from the space; the timbre and tone of the sound in the space all combine to create a rather indelible image of a place in our memory. The care and skill of the interior designer enhances these experiences for all of us. The function, safety and value of the spaces created are equally as important as the aesthetics of the space. Like all environmental designers, interior designers are engaged in complex work combining both science and art.

Figure 3.65 . . .

A dining hall at Queens College Oxford. The model for the dining room of Hogworts in the Harry Potter movies.

As buildings became more and more complex and our demands for function and beauty ever more stringent, designers that liked to work in these areas began to find enough work to support separate design businesses. Interior design today is a thriving design field with much of its work being done in commercial interiors. Contrary to what we might see today on Home and Garden television, most interior design work is not in the residential setting although that area of work is still very important.

Interior designers have been fighting for many years to become equal partners in the environmental design fields. Their desires are entirely legitimate and their value unmistakable. One problem area for the field has been to get beyond their history of growing up as a part of the home economics programs in most universities around the United States. Many interior design programs have moved out of the home-ec departments and joined the design colleges. This integration is positive for interior design and for the rest of the environmental design fields. A part of this recognition, of the importance of interior design, is the move to require licensure for interior designers. Several states now require licensure for interior designers but several do not. The work toward licensure is still ongoing and is something that all environmental designers should be pushing.

Interior design work is about creating spaces that optimize our functioning within those spaces while bringing a sense of emotional and aesthetic connection to those spaces. Like all environmental design fields, interior design is about solving problems. The problems here involve a smaller scale of spaces and require a more in-depth knowledge of those spaces and their functioning. Interior designers must have a thorough understanding of the materials involved including their durability, their reactions to fire, the sustainability of their production processes, their origin, manufacture, and ultimate recyclability. They also must be knowledgeable about the latest in anthropometrics, color theory, lighting, physical comfort, noise control, acoustic reinforcement, and a host of other technical subjects that make our interior spaces both functional and special.

Interior design practices are often split between residential interiors work and commercial interiors work. Some interior design firms do both types of work but others choose to specialize. Following is a brief description of the types of work being done in each of these areas.

Figure 3.66 . . .

The music room in the "House for an Art Lover" by Charles Renee Macintosh and his wife Margaret MacDonald.

Figure 3.67 . . .

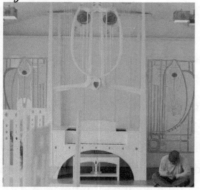

The custom designed piano for the music room in the "House for an Art Lover."

# RESIDENTIAL INTERIORS

Residential interiors are probably the most intimate spaces designed by environmental designers. The interior designer works very, very closely with the occupants of the home to determine their needs, their wishes, their style of living, and their preferences. They must then meld together these often disparate ideas to create wonderful spaces in which we live our lives. The hallmark of interior design work is in efficient functioning of the spaces, but also in the degree of detail in the materials and construction that communicate the values and dreams of the inhabitants.

The music room in the home, shown left, is a collaboration between an architect, Charles Renee Macintosh and an interior designer and artist Margaret MacDonald, his wife.

The entire room is a custom-designed and fabricated interior. The fireplace, drapery panels at the French doors, and even the piano were designed by the husband and wife team. This is a good indication of the level of detail and finish that is often incorporated into a residential interior design project. The picture of the interior of the Robie House (Figure 3.68), by Frank Lloyd Wright, shows this same level of care and concern for the detail of the interior including ceiling moldings, mechanical vents and stained glass in the French doors. This is also an example of an interior done by an architect not an interior designer. There is a fair amount of cross-over between these two fields and many architecture firms include interior designers in their firms. Historically architects often designed their own interiors but the modern real estate market and the complexity of materials has made it much more difficult for an architect to commit the time necessary to do interiors as well as architecture.

With the huge market in upscale high-rise condominiums in most of our large cities, the interior designers are busy helping owners define their own particular lifestyle. They also design model units for the real estate developers to help potential owners picture the possibilities of their new condo.

Residential interior design has been a very busy segment of the environmental design fields during this recent housing boom. The residential part of the business is however, subject to the cyclical nature of real estate development. At this time we are seeing a pretty marked decrease in the number of housing units being built in the

Figure 3.68 . . .

The living room wall in the Robie House in Chicago
by Frank Lloyd Wright.

Figure 3.69 . . .

A model condominium unit in the St. Regis tower
in downtown San Francisco.

country, and therefore the potential work for residential interior designers will also lag. This is true of all of the environmental design fields although not all segments of the industry rise and fall in the same pattern. This is one reason that so many design firms offer all of the environmental design specialties within their firm. It makes the ups and downs a little bit easier to handle.

## COMMERCIAL INTERIORS

Commercial interiors include three somewhat separate areas of design work. The office/retail segment, interiors for public buildings, and special purpose interiors each require a certain degree of special knowledge and experience. Most commercial interior design firms do not specialize in just one of these areas, they tend to do work in all three. Commercial interiors involving office space challenge the designer to create efficient working conditions with good lighting, temperature control and good acoustics. An efficient and pleasant work environment has been the bread and butter of commercial office interiors for many years. With the help of behavioral scientists and business researchers, we have been finding that we can create spaces that are too efficient. Spaces that are ultra efficient do not allow people to just run into each other and talk about what they are doing and maybe just find out that they can help each other out or find the next great idea. Office design today involves creating opportunities for chance encounters and sharing information in ways that were not even dreamed of five years ago.

Retail shopping spaces are also included in this category of interior design work. Since our society has moved toward shopping as an entertainment experience there has been tremendous pressure put on the design of those retail spaces. Retail spaces are now about creating excitement or relaxation or some other mood to serve the selling of goods. Theme retail is particularly huge for interior designers now. Just look at the "Where The Wild Things Are" photo on the following page. This is not your usual store. It is part entertainment, part adventure and part retail based on the popular children's book by Maurice Sendak. These themed retail spaces are very popular

Figure 3.70 . . .

A retail shopping interior modeled after the Galleria in Milan. The Gavidae Shopping Center in Minneapolis.

Figure 3.71 . . .

A *Where The Wild Things Are* entertainment and retail experience inside the Metreon in San Francisco.

Figure 3.72 . . .

An inventive shading device in the Salt Lake City Public Library.

but they also loose their attraction fairly quickly and need to be redesigned to remain successful. The "Wild Things" are no longer cavorting around the Metreon. The space is now something else.

The sophistication of retail marketing has increased and increased in the past decade. Interior designers are paying much more attention to complex and dramatic lighting systems, surround sound systems, color, and even the distribution of smells in the spaces they design for retail.

The public building category includes any interiors in government buildings such as city halls, convention centers, libraries, or school building interiors. These types of buildings provide interior spaces for large numbers of people, often in big gatherings, and require a certain type of sensibility and attention to detail. One area of increased focus for interior designers is in building security. It has become a pretty major issue for public building interiors. Demand for natural lighting and passive energy control have also added new challenges to the interior designers work. The photograph below of the Salt Lake Library show a unique strategy for shading the lower level children's book area when the sun is streaming in the huge windows. It not only looks great but it works and solves a comfort problem and a material degradation problem for the library and its patrons. Other types of projects in this category might include museums or laboratories where the control of light and heat is critical. Interior designers work closely with architects and other environmental designers on most projects but probably most closely on public projects.

Specialty interior design includes project types that require very specialized knowledge and experience to be completed successfully. A theater with its focus on sight and sound requires a very special knowledge based in acoustics, lighting, theater arts, and even set design to be able to incorporate all of the necessary elements into the space. The new theater at the Guthrie in Minneapolis is a good example of a very complex

Figure 3.73 . . .

The Student Services Building at the University of Utah. A very constrained but impressive interior to serve the needs of the student body at the university.

Figure 3.74 . . .

The main thrust stage theater at the new Guthrie Theater Complex in Minneapolis.

Figure 3.75 . . .

Historic renovation. The Musee d'Orsay in Paris after it was converted from a train station into a major art museum. The interior designer was Gae Aulenti.

theater space that gives theatergoers a unique set of possibilities for watching plays and very sophisticated and unique ways for the theater company to present plays.

Other specialty interiors might include historic preservation or re-use such as the re-use of the Gare d'Orsay train station as a museum to hold and display the impressionist collection of the French government. This is a great project visited and enjoyed by hundreds of thousands of people a year. The design of an airplane interior, the interior of a boat or even the interior of a space station provide very unique challenges for interior designers.

## ORGANIZATION OF INTERIOR DESIGN FIRMS

Interior designers work in a wide variety of settings. Many interior designers work for private consulting firms that specialize in interior design or for multi-discipline design firms that offer services in interior design, architecture, landscape architecture, urban design and planning. Multi-discipline design firms support the idea that I have been trying to promote here—that environmental design is really one large profession with a group of specialties within it. Other interior designers may find themselves working in corporate offices providing design services for the thousands of employees in their company. Or they may find themselves working for large retail stores designing and re-designing the stores and displays. Some may even work for large furniture retailers who like to provide interior design services along with the furniture for business or residential customers. Whatever the organization, interior designers have many choices in how they utilize their skills and education.

## THE EDUCATION OF AN INTERIOR DESIGNER

Interior designers are moving toward having a comprehensive licensing law in the United States but they are not there yet. In lieu of licensing, interior designers are encouraged by their professional organizations to become qualified through the National Council for Interior Design Qualification (NCIDQ) which includes documenting education, experience and passing a rigorous examination. The process is very similar to licensing in architecture and landscape architecture. The educational requirement is a Bachelor's Degree in Interior Design from a university with a program accredited by the Foundation for Interior Design Education and Research (FIDER).

Bachelor of Interior Design programs are typically a four-year degree program although some may be five years in duration.

Although an individual may practice interior design in many states without a license, it is highly recommended that one studies at an accredited program and seeks qualification through NCIDQ. Society will be served better by having interior design professionals with the proper education and experience. Students will be better served as well.

# Engineering

The engineering fields are incredibly important to environmental design. Without the technical expertise of various engineers the work we do to design and build our environment could not be done. That being said, I do not include engineers in the group of disciplines we are calling the environmental design fields. The primary reason for this is that engineers are trained primarily in the science side of the environmental design equation and receive little if any education in the artistic or design side of the equation. Earlier in this book the concepts of thinking styles was presented. We all utilize various styles of thinking in our daily lives but we tend to prefer one type of thinking. By the nature of an engineers educational system, those people that prefer to think in a more global, visionary way, or with a focus on people find themselves ill-suited for engineering. Those individuals that favor fact-based, logical, and linear decision-making processes are likely to be successful in engineering.

I see some acknowledgement of these shortcomings within the engineering disciplines and also see some changes occurring in their educational strategy. I think that engineers that deal with buildings and the environment should be fully participating members of the environmental design professions, and I hope that my evaluation can change over the next few years. One of the changes that I see in our future is that engineering degrees will be extended from the current four year degrees to five year professional degrees similar to landscape architecture and architecture. This will give engineering educators the opportunity to build more design into their programs as well as deal with the ever increasing amount of technical knowledge necessary.

The most successful engineers that I know and have worked with are visionary thinkers and do care about the impact of their work on people. They are open to the possibility that inspiration to solve a problem may come from the most unlikely places. Quite a few of these types of engineers find their way into multi-discipline environmental design firms and fill very valuable roles in those firms.

Below, I will describe the relationships between engineering and environmental design for the five most common types of engineering used in environmental design projects. There are many additional types of engineers, but these five are the ones that work most closely with environmental designers.

Figure 3.76 . . .

The Duluth Lift Bridge, a great old piece of civil engineering that has become the icon of the city of Duluth, Minnesota.

## CIVIL/STRUCTURAL ENGINEERING

Civil and structural engineers are typically educated as structural specialists within civil engineering. The civil engineering side of their work is concerned with the creation of roadways, bridges, pipelines, and other parts of the infrastructure system of our world. Civil engineering is traditionally thought of as utilitarian and functional only, but I think we all recognize when we see a bridge, that not only functions but is beautiful as well. There is a lot of room for beauty in engineering.

Figure 3.77...

The structure of a high-rise building under construction in Chicago.

Figure 3.78...

The integrated structure of the United Terminal at O'Hare Airport.

Figure 3.79...

The structural part of engineering is certainly incredibly important to environmental design, particularly architecture. The structural engineers work with architects to make sure that the buildings can stand up and withstand the forces of nature. We need to support our own weight as well as the weight of the building but also the weight of the things we pack into buildings and the snow and ice that settle on the buildings in winter. We also need to withstand the forces of wind on a building or the forces of an earthquake. These are formidable tasks that the structural engineer is responsible for. Most often the work of the structural engineer is hidden inside the walls, floors and ceilings of our buildings. We don't get the chance to really see and understand the complex systems that helps us to build our environment. Figure 3.77 is a picture of the USG building in Chicago while it was under construction. The massive steel frame is visible now but starting to be covered up. The structural developments of engineers have allowed incredible advances in our ability to create large, more complex and more robust buildings. The frame that you see allows us to build high into the air while keeping major portions of the outside of the building open to allow views and day-lighting to enter the building.

In the modernist tradition, structural engineering can become an important part of the decoration of a building. In the United Terminal at O'Hare Airport the architect and engineer, both working within the same design firm, carefully coordinated the engineering of the structure and its visual look and feel to create an engaging and light look for the entire building. Notice both the amount of glass in the structure and also the holes cut in the structural beams which lets them look and feel light and airy. The holes are not hampering the structural integrity of the building, in fact they cut down on the weight of the building.

We often rely on structural engineers to provide the WOW factor in our buildings. The engineers of the Guthrie Theater complex in Minneapolis designed a structure that allows for a public lounge and viewing platform to cantilever well beyond the edge of the building as it hangs over and looks at the Mississippi River. This is probably one of the largest cantilevers in the world and it is impressive.

Civil/structural engineers are essential team members in any environmental design project. Their contributions are critical and I would like to find ways to align them even more closely with the whole environmental design field in education and experience. They are so important to our continuing ability to design and construct sustainable projects.

The truly amazing structural cantilever of the Guthrie Theater complex in Minneapolis, Minnesota.

# MECHANICAL ENGINEERING

Mechanical engineering, as it applies to environmental design, includes the design of heating, ventilating, and air conditioning (HVAC) systems for buildings and the design of all of the plumbing necessary to allow a building to function. Mechanical engineers are key partners in the quest to create much more sustainable buildings that utilize much less energy and maybe even make energy. Mechanical engineers have for so many years, been focused on the active systems to heat and cool and ventilate a building. Now they are being asked to provide systems that take advantage of the natural world around us and reduce energy consumption dramatically. Some of the new strategies for heating and cooling buildings including ground source heat pumps are pretty remarkable. This system uses the stable temperature of the earth to either heat or cool a building. It requires much less energy to run than traditional systems and therefore generates less pollution. Working with landscape architects, mechanical engineers are finding ways to use plants inside buildings to filter air, scrub carbon dioxide out of the air and to provide oxygen to our buildings. These processes require much less energy than bringing air in from outside the building and either heating or cooling it.

Mechanical engineers have also been pushing developments in plumbing that are also much more sustainable than the systems used in the past. Collection and re-use of grey water saves millions of gallons of water a year. This water can be easily filtered and used again to water plant materials on the site or to flush toilets. Even sewage treatment is changing as environmental scientists and landscape architects work with mechanical engineers to find more sustainable ways to treat the effluent from our buildings.

The work of mechanical engineers is usually hidden behind the skin of a building or under the floor or above the ceiling. It is not often viewed by people in our buildings. The Pompidou Center in Paris is a really interesting example of a building that wears all of the mechanical and electrical systems on the outside of the building. This was done to keep the interior of this huge art museum and research center as free and flexible as possible while allowing for maintenance of the systems without disrupting the activities inside. You can see here the heating and cooling ducts, the building piping, electrical conduits, elevators, etc. on the outside of the building.

Since mechanical engineers also work to create machines that meet the needs of people, they are often called upon to help architects, and other engineers to create machines that provide services for buildings. The Institute de Monde Arabe in Paris by architect Jean Nouvel utilizes an animated screen on the south facing façade of the building

*Figure 3.80 . . .*

The mechanical and electrical systems create the decoration on the outside of the building at the Pompidou Center in Paris.

to block the harsh and hot sun. The circular openings in the screen contain iris lenses that look like a camera lens. When the sun is bright on the building a photo sensor closes the iris lenses to keep the sun from getting into the building. When it is not sunny the lenses open back up. It is very unique to sit in the plaza and watch the side of the building change. Also shown in Figure 3.82 is a weather vane at the Science Museum of Glasgow, Scotland. This structure is a really good visual example of the coordination between structural engineering, mechanical engineering and architecture. The tower rotates in the wind to mark the winds direction but it also has an elevator in it and an observation room at the top of the tower.

Figure 3.81 . . .

The sun shading screen on the south façade of the Institute de Monde Arabe in Paris.

Figure 3.82 . . .

A rather large weather vane at the Science Museum in Glasgow, Scotland.

# ELECTRICAL ENGINEERING

Electrical engineering is a very broad field that includes the design of computers, integrated circuits, chips, radio frequency devices, etc. The list of things an electrical engineer could be involved in goes on and on. The portions of electrical engineering that are most closely associated with environmental design are those areas tied to building. The electrical engineer will be involved in designing the systems that are providing power to a project, artificial lighting to a project, and communications to the project.

The idea that an electrical engineer is in charge of providing power to our buildings and spaces seems pretty simple and straightforward. Just look around you. How many pieces of equipment do you see that need power? How many things do you hear in the background that are heating or cooling the room? Think about how vulnerable we feel when the power goes out and we can't do our work or be easily entertained. The amount of power used within our built environment is staggering. The electrical engineer is charged with providing the power to heat and cool our spaces, to run all the equipment that we have, and to do so in a way that we are not really aware of it. It is not an easy job.

Providing lighting to our buildings, cities and landscapes is also a charge given to electrical engineers. We are certainly no longer limited to daylight hours to live our lives thanks to the electric light. We have come to rely on artificial lighting too much. Both environmental designers and electrical engineers are working to reduce our reliance on artificial lighting as much as possible. We still use a lot of electricity for lighting, but engineers are developing more efficient bulbs and lighting strategies that allow us to conserve a great deal of energy.

Communications is also an area where electrical engineers contribute a great deal of knowledge and expertise to environmental design. Less than a century ago, the only communication systems we had to deal with were telephone, the radio and face to face talking. Now the electrical engineers are challenged by needing to coordinate telephone networks, video networks, radio networks, and miles and miles of data networks both wired and wireless. These are the most obvious communication systems in our built environment, but the engineers must also provide communication systems dedicated to safety and security such as fire alarm and suppression systems, security and even global positioning systems linked to satellites.

Electrical engineers are also involved with the generation of power for our use. This is an area of work where the ideals of sustainability, that are so important to environmental designers, can be utilized by the engineers to have tremendous impact on our world. Engineers are being challenged to create electricity in ways that are sustainable for the future. Renewable resources of power such as wind and sun are developing rapidly thanks to the research efforts of many electrical engineers.

## GEOTECHNICAL ENGINEERING

Geotechnical engineers work most closely with civil/structural engineers, architects and occasionally landscape architects. They explore and test the underlying geology of an area or specific site. They provide important information about the form of the geology, and its capacity to support the proposed uses on the land. This includes information about sub-soil drainage, sub-surface water, strength and composition of the soil and sub-surface and the stability of the area over time.

## ENVIRONMENTAL ENGINEERING

As the impacts of human habitation on our planet become more and more apparent, we turn to environmental engineers to help us understand the processes being impacted. The health of the environment is their primary concern. Their work is used by planners and landscape architects extensively as we try to determine the past impacts we have had on the land and how we might address positive change. We also utilize their expertise to determine the potential impact of development on the natural systems of the environment. Most major projects are required to prepare an "environmental impact statement" to determine whether or not a proposed project can be compatible with the natural environment and ultimately whether it should be allowed to continue.

# Related Design Specialties

Each of the following groups of people are involved with environmental designers in limited but important ways. Environmental designers will typically contract with or consult with them on individual projects as needed. Each of them provides services, knowledge and expertise important to creating the best environments that we can.

## ENVIRONMENTAL ARTISTS

The specific area of environmental art is a sub-set of artists whose work is designed as an integral part of our built environment. Their work ranges from projects that are objects in the environment like Robert Smithson's Spiral Jetty in the Great Salt Lake or Cristo's Umbrellas that dotted the landscape in California and Japan, to projects that are integral to the built environment like the two shown on the right.

The entry court at the new deYoung Museum is an environmental sculpture by Andy Goldworthy. It includes large stones and paving with cracks running through the work that help direct visitors into and out of the building. The cracks provide a memory link to the Loma Prieta earthquake of 1989 which was the reason for building a new museum. The connecting tunnel between terminals at the United Terminal at O'Hare Airport is an example of architecture, interior design, art and music coming together to create a singular and unique experience. The rather bland act of moving through a very long tunnel is enhanced by a kinetic neon sculpture that runs the length of the space. In addition we are treated to a piece of music written specifically for our movement through the space.

Figure 3.83 . . .

The entry court at the deYoung Museum in San Francisco. Sculpture by Andy Goldworthy.

## BUILDING MATERIAL SUPPLIERS

In order to keep abreast of the incredible developments in building materials, equipment, furniture, and plant materials, environmental designers rely heavily on those people and companies that develop and produce products for the field. Companies are constantly developing new and better materials. It is very hard for environmental designers to keep up with all of the developments. It is exciting when someone brings a new material or a new product into the office.

Figure 3.84 . . .

The tunnel connecting terminals at the O'Hare Airport United Airlines Terminal.

It is up to the environmental designer to evaluate that product and make sure that it works well for their projects, but without the suppliers we would not be able to keep up. Much of the positive development in sustainable materials and sustainable systems is being developed by private companies. They undertake this product development work as a response to the needs of the environmental designers.

## BEHAVIORAL SCIENTISTS

Why would I include behavioral scientists in this list? Behavioral scientists are continually involved in research that gives us new and better information about how we use and respond to our environment. New developments in network theory may lead to better planning strategies. New understanding of human behavior in a panic state will lead to better and safer buildings, and new knowledge about how we perceive the world may allow environmental designers to do a better job of creating that world.

# PART 4

# The Act of Design

## INTRODUCTION

*D*esign is a very wonderful and mysterious process to be involved in. Design is not well understood by the public and when asked to describe what they do, many environmental designers have difficulty answering the question. They often insist that they just do it. They don't really know specifically what it is that they do. The mystery lies in two aspects of design. First, the fact that design is not a linear process like most of the things that we have learned in our lives and second, the use of drawings as a communicative tool.

Figure 4.1 . . .

The Salt Lake City Library under construction. Moshe Safdie, FAIA.

Many things that we do in our lives involve steps in a given order—like putting a bicycle together, connect part A to part B with bolt C. Design is not like that, it is not a rote, linear process which is why it is so mysterious to so many people. It involves the exploration of myriad possibilities, many of which can solve the problem. Artificial intelligence researchers label design as a "wicked problem" because of the almost infinite number of possibilities to be considered in the resolution of the design problem, and the fact that there is seldom one correct answer to the problem. Successful designers are not afraid to work in this kind of limbo and are not afraid to take risks in solving these wicked problems. They are not afraid to try things that have never been done before.

The act of design does not always have to be so mysterious and our understanding of design begins with our ability to recognize very simple building blocks that exist in almost everything that is designed. This part of the book introduces each of these simple building blocks of design and sends you on an adventure to find them in your own environment. Creating environments for people and other living things is an extremely complex undertaking, but it begins with very simple ideas that are combined over and over again into much more complex notions and environments. The introduction of these simple building blocks should probably take you back to kindergarten, which is where you first saw and heard about many of these ideas.

As a side note: a large part of being a designer is getting in touch with the feelings of wonder that you experienced as a child. Children are incredibly perceptive about the environment around them. They are constantly asking questions and wondering. These are excellent characteristics for any environmental designer.

The other mystery in environmental design involves the use of a different language than that used by a majority of our society. The design language is drawing. Drawing is one of the most effective ways we have to explore design problems and to communicate ideas about our three dimensional world. Drawing empowers designers because it is a form of communication that a great number of people do not understand and find very mysterious. The public is in awe of a person that can draw and that can find meaning in drawings. At times, the mysterious nature of drawing serves to make environmental designers unique. The necessity to draw means that not everyone can do the work that environmental designers do. We guard our ability to draw, to speak this unique language so that we continue to be unique. At other times, the mysterious nature of drawing serves to alienate us from the people that we are trying to serve. A very large part of an environmental designers work is to communicate the design ideas generated to clients and the public. Educating people to read drawings and not to be fearful of them becomes one task that is essential for environmental design professionals. Drawing, sketching, and exploring ideas within a visual language are activities that all of you should be engaged in on a daily basis. As you read Part 4, *The Act of Design*, you will be asked to go out into the world around you and find examples of the ideas that are being presented in the text. You should not only locate them but draw a sketch of them in a sketchbook that is your constant companion. Train your eye to see in an analytical fashion and train your hand to describe those things that the eye sees. The ability to draw and sketch for an environmental designer expands their ability to explore ideas and to communicate with their clients and the public in a much better way than using only words. I would suggest that the old adage "a picture is worth a thousand words" is doubly true in the environmental design fields.

One of the comments that I receive all the time as an environmental design educator and practitioner is that design is subjective. How in the world can we identify "good" design when it is such a subjective thing? What one person likes is so different from what someone else likes. Design projects are evaluated on many different scales, only some of which are subjective. The finished products of design are indeed the result of solving the "wicked problem" in the best way possible. The evaluation of the success or failure of the solution is not as simple as saying "I like it" or "I hate it." Environmental designers must consider many different issues when designing their solution and so evaluation of that solution must also take into account multiple criteria. The following list contains a possible list of criteria for evaluating an environmental design project. This is not an exhaustive list.

1. The results of our design efforts must meet the functional needs of the people that use the space.

2. The project should be sensitive to its context.

3. The project should establish its own unique place in space and time.

4. The project should be substantial and resist the aging effects of our environment.

5. The project should fit into the world's systems and be sensitive to our environment.

6. The project should do no harm.

7. The project should establish a connection with people's emotions and feelings.

8. The project should be furthering the intellectual discourse in environmental design.

Successfully meeting all of these criteria is very difficult. It takes a great deal of education and experience to produce good design work. Using scales such as these we can begin to rank environmental design work as to which is better than the other, but we will never be able to say that one project is the best or that one solution is the one single correct answer. Each individual designer, or more appropriately design team, will come up with a different solution to the same problem. Throughout Part 4 I have tried to use examples of environmental design projects that are successful in meeting many of the above criteria to illustrate the basic building blocks of environmental design. If you find an image that piques your interest, please look up the project or the designer in the library or on-line.

In our brief look at the "act of design" we will start with an exploration of the educational process used to train and empower new designers. We will then introduce the fundamental building blocks used in the environmental design fields, along with the primary means of organizing the elements of environmental design.

Figure 4.2 . . .

The entry space of the Milwaukee Art Museum by Santiago Calatrava.

# The Basic Design Language

Environmental designers, regardless of their specific discipline, are referred to as design professionals. The word "professional" is not used lightly. It means that the people involved have specific and technical knowledge in their field and that they are responsible for the safety and well being of the public that they serve. As mentioned earlier in this book, professionals usually must hold a license to practice in their discipline. Licenses are granted by each individual state after completion of educational requirements, internship requirements and passing a nationally administered test in your area of environmental design. Each different environmental design field has specific requirements for how much and what type of education and internship experience you must have to be licensed. Again, the specifics of education and licensure were discussed previously in Part 3.

Design education is the first step in this rather long process of becoming an environmental designer. From the start of your education to receiving your license you may invest anywhere from seven to ten years of your life. A college degree from an accredited university is required in any of the environmental design fields. The degrees may vary from a four year bachelor's degree, to a five year bachelor's degree or to a six or seven year master's degree. All of these degree programs share a great deal of common knowledge and information. It is this common knowledge that we are most concerned about in this part of the book. It is advantageous for an environmental designer to be a generalist first and a specialist second. Environmental designers all share the design process as a fundamental building block of their knowledge. They also share the language of drawing. All environmental designers must learn a great deal about each other's fields so that they will be able to communicate effectively with each other as they form teams of designers to solve a given design problem. While their generalist knowledge allows them to communicate more effectively and to be more flexible in their thinking, their special knowledge in their chosen environmental design field allows them to master a part of this very complex endeavor, the design of our environment.

Amassing this general environmental design knowledge starts with building a working design language, both visual and verbal. We begin by training the senses to become more aware and more acute. We train the eyes to see in a new way, with more detail and more wonder. We develop new appreciation for the smells of a place or the texture of a material used. We feel the texture of the world around us. We look for the order, the disorder, the meaning in our environment, whether man-made or natural. As our senses become more aware, we attach words to our new experiences and knowledge. Many new words will be introduced in this book and in any environmental design course. (Please take the time to look up a word if you do not know its meaning.) The more accurately we can communicate, both visually and verbally (which includes writing) the richer our environments can become. The next piece of shared design knowledge acquired in our environmental design education are the principles of basic design. These principles apply to the arts as well as all of the environmental design fields.

I have dedicated this part of this book to the introduction of these principles of basic design. As design educators, we try to build your design language with words and pictures, but the most effective way to understand these principles is to seek them out in the real world. Go out and find examples of each of the principles and sketch them. You will understand the principle better and you will be training your eyes and hands to communicate using drawings.

A large part of your education in an environmental design field will be spent acquiring specific technical knowledge applicable to the field of your choice. As an example, interior designers must gain specific knowledge about the materials they will use. To even pick a wall covering you will have to know the flammability of the material, the off-gassing tendencies of the material, where it came from and how using it might affect the quality of our larger environment, the colorfastness of the material, how the material ages, etc. A landscape architect will want to know which type of plant will survive in the specific type of soil and climate, the growth characteristics of the plant, the changing colors of the plant throughout the seasons, the diseases the plant might be susceptible to, the compatibility of the plant with other plants, the drainage of the area, etc. Each of the environmental design fields have courses in their degree programs that focus on the technical knowledge specific to that field. Design education also involves practicing what you have learned in the design studio. Design studio is the place where the aesthetics of design, the technology of your chosen field, and real problem-solving come together. Design studio is an equal partner in environmental design education with the technical information courses you will take. We will cover the nature of the design studio in more detail a little later.

Design education, like most things, is a life-long endeavor. We will never know enough about what we do, about our environment, about architecture, interior design, landscape architecture, urban design, or planning. This fact is very appealing to many of us. The environmental design fields never have to be boring. It is up to each one of us to be committed to learning more; to improving our own abilities; to improving as designers. To paraphrase a comment by Douglas Cardinal in a speech to the Department of Architecture and Landscape Architecture at North Dakota State University in 1994: it is each designers challenge to fly like an eagle in the black abyss of the unknown. Your chance for improvement never stops and each new design problem is different from the last one. Design is also a serious and meaningful endeavor. The quality of our built environment is in our hands. I would suggest that we have not done a very good job in the last 50 years. There is a great deal of room for improvement. Environmental design is a passionate challenge.

Figure 4.3 . . .

An urban design studio at North Dakota State University. The model is of Winnipeg, Manitoba.

Figure 4.4 . . .

An architectural design studio at North Dakota State University.

Figure 4.5 . . .

A studio in an architectural office in Fargo.

# THE DESIGN STUDIO

The design studio is a physical place to work used in both the design schools and in the design professionals' offices. It is a place where a group of designers can work on their design problems, learning from each other, and facilitating a free flow of ideas back and forth. Design is best accomplished in the presence of others, in a place where you can discuss the possibilities and the options that you face. Within the design studio, teams of designers from different design fields might be assembled to tackle one specific design problem. A team is usually assembled for each design project that is undertaken by the firm. A single environmental designer might actually be asked to be a member on more than one team, depending on the time commitment needed. Individuals may be working on separate problems also in the same studio setting. Design teams in environmental design firms usually disband at the end of a project with team members moving to different projects that require their particular set of skills and insights. The studio, as a space for working and solving problems, develops a highly charged intellectual atmosphere that not only contributes to the solution of the problems undertaken, but also invigorates and sustains the people that work within it. Studios tend to be light-filled, colorful, active spaces whether they are located in the countryside, or in the urban core. The studio is a very important part of the working process, the act of design, for environmental designers.

The design studio is not only a place, but also the designation given a series of courses in environmental design programs at the university. Studio is the core of any environmental design curriculum. Students usually have a design studio each semester they are enrolled in school. The design studio is the course in which you bring all of your knowledge together to solve the problems assigned by the faculty. Your basic design knowledge, your drawing skills, your technical knowledge all come together in studio. Design studios in school take a tremendous amount of time and commitment. In most design schools, studios are open 24 hours a day 365 days a year. It is not uncommon to find students in studio at 3 o'clock in the morning working on a design problem. It may be a disservice to students and professionals to encourage these types of work habits, but then design is not like other forms of problem solving. Creativity is not a function that can be turned on at 8:00 am and turned off at 5:00 pm. The flexibility of the design studio is very important to the design process.

Environmental design fields seem to require a highly developed ego in its practioners. I think this is true because of the personal, intellectual risk that is involved in design. It is very much related to the eagle flying in the black abyss. It takes courage to place one of your ideas in front of other people and ask them to criticize it. A strong sense of self in an environmental designer is a good thing, but . . . we also must realize that environmental design is almost always accomplished by a team of designers from different fields working together on a common goal.

During the education of an environmental designer we hope to both bolster your ego and make you a better team player. Design education also develops your visual and verbal language while giving you the technical and aesthetic skills necessary to make environmental spaces and to judge the relative success of those environments.

# Chapter 14

## Basic Design Elements in Environmental Design

Designers involved in the fields of environmental design are concerned with the three dimensional world. Our world has width, depth and height. The study of the basic design elements that we use, however, starts with a non-dimensional element (the point), and builds our understanding through the introduction of two dimensional elements (line and plane), three dimensional elements (volume and space) and insists that we understand the fourth dimension (time and motion) as it impacts our three dimensional world. To be successful designers of the built environment we must master these basic elements of design.

Figure 4.6 . . .

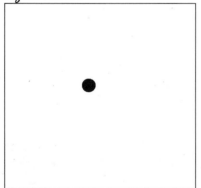

A point in space.

Figure 4.7 . . .

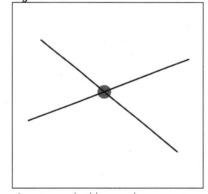

A point marked by two lines crossing.

Figure 4.8 . . .

A single tree marking a point in the landscape.

## POINT

The term "point" in the dictionary takes up over 6-1/2 column inches of definitions, none of which adequately defines "point" as used in the design fields. A point marks position, it is a visual focus. A point can also be defined as the spot at which two lines cross. We understand the intersection of two roads in the city to be a particular place. The intersection is a point in the landscape for us to take our bearings. Theoretically, a point has no dimension. It has no length, width, or depth. It is an abstract idea, a concept. But the way that we use "point" in environmental design is anything but abstract. We mark points in our environment with real things, built or natural. A single tree marks a spot, providing focus; an obelisk places emphasis on a singular spot in our urban environment; a sculpture focuses an interior space; or an umbrella sets apart a space in the environment making it more prominent than other spaces. The tree shown in Figure 4.8 marks a particular place in a vast landscape. Parts of the Great Plains are seemingly unending and flat. Without the tree to let us know where we are in the vastness, our wanderings on the plains would be very frightening. New technology brings even more importance to our understanding of points on the earth. Global Positioning Systems (GPS) can identify points accurately on the globe within a few feet. The tree in the photograph is located at Latitude 46.782341N and Longitude 96.900131W.

Figure 4.9 . . .

The Washington Monument in Washington, D.C. Marking a particular place in the city and focusing us on a particular person in our history.

Figure 4.10 . . .

A sculpture as a focal point at Place de la Republique, Paris.

Figure 4.11 . . .

One of Cristo's Umbrellas marking a point in Southern California.

Figure 4.12 . . .

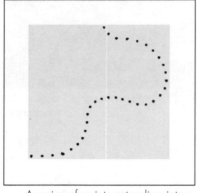

A series of points extending into a line.

Figure 4.13 . . .

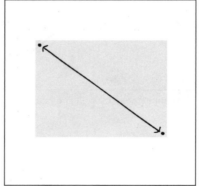

Visually connecting two points creates a line.

Figure 4.14 . . .

The Mall in Washington, D.C. A visually implied line connecting the Lincoln Memorial with the Washington Monument and the U.S. Capitol.

# LINE

Again speaking theoretically, a line is an abstract idea with only one dimension: length. Lines are constructed from points, either by connecting two or more points or by extension of the point. The lines that we find in environmental design are both real and implied. The Mall in Washington, D.C. implies a line from the Capitol to the Washington Monument and on to the Lincoln Memorial. This line in the city is an important axis for the organization of the entire city. Real lines abound in the environment; streets and rivers are but two easily identifiable examples.

Lines have a number of physical characteristics.

- Lines have prominent length, thinness and narrow breadth.

- Lines imply direction. A line may physically end but it has the power to imply continuation and direction. A line points to something or to somewhere.

- Lines can be straight, curved, regular, irregular, bent and warped.

- Lines can have parallel edges or non-parallel edges.

Lines show up in architecture as such things as columns, circulation or cornices. They show up in the landscape as rivers or canals, or walkways. They show up in interiors as wall trim, ceiling grids, handrails. They show up in urban settings as streets, sidewalks, axis, etc. The line is a very simple and very effective tool for an environmental designer.

Figure 4.15 . . .

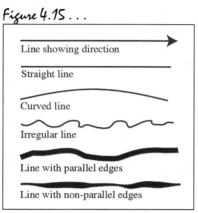

Various lines and their characteristics.

Figure 4.16 . . .

The Red River of the North in Fargo, North Dakota. A meandering, natural line in our landscape.

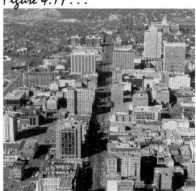

Figure 4.17 . . .

The streets of Salt Lake City, Utah. Straight lines in the landscape that organize the city and serve transportation.

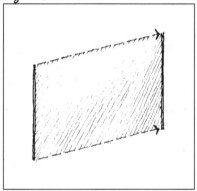

Figure 4.18 . . .

A line moved through space describes a plane.

## PLANE

The "plane" in environmental design is a two dimensional element. It has width and length but no depth. Again we are speaking theoretically since a plane of real material must have some depth. A plane is formed by extending a line through space. Planes can also be said to be bordered by lines. As we view a plane we see the edge of the plane as a line. This is particularly true when we draw a representation of a plane. We draw a line around the extent of the plane, differentiating the plane from its surroundings. A plane can also be implied in environmental design with a series of lines related to one another. An arcade of columns in a Greek Temple implies an exterior plane. A windrow of trees on the prairie implies a plane on the land.

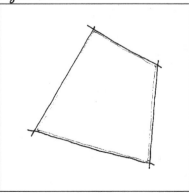

Figure 4.19 . . .

We can describe a plane by drawing four lines that bound the plane.

Figure 4.20 . . .

A colonnade, a series of columns, used to imply a plane in space.

Figure 4.21 . . .

A natural but man-made plane in the landscape. A windrow in Eastern North Dakota.

Figure 4.22 . . .

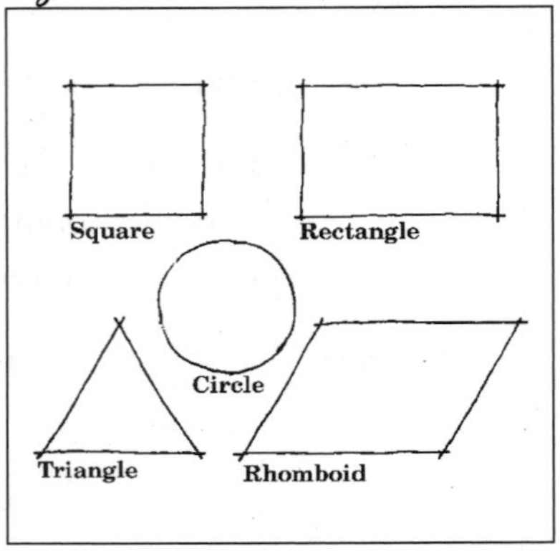

Geometric planar elements.

Figure 4.23 . . .

A memorial designed almost entirely of planes in the landscape. The Vietnam War Memorial in Washington, D.C. by Maya Lin.

A plane, whether real or implied, can be regular or irregular, and flat or warped. Squares, rectangles, triangles, circles, and rhomboids are regular geometric planar elements that we learned about in kindergarten. R. Buckminster Fuller combined a series of flat triangular planes to create the geodesic dome, a curved plane. Planes can also be irregular and warped such as a leaf, a crumpled sheet of aluminum foil or a sculptural roof plane.

Planes are a basic design element used extensively in environmental design. They can be oriented in any direction relative to our world. We most often see them oriented horizontally (such as roof planes, ceiling planes, or floor planes) or vertically (such as walls). One of the most powerful uses of the plane in recent history is in the walls of the Vietnam War Memorial in Washington, D.C. designed by Maya Lin. One very simple vertical plane is hinged in the middle and placed on a sloping

Figure 4.24 . . .

Furniture as planes. The Red-Blue Chair designed by Garrit Rietveld in 1918.

Figure 4.25 . . .

Architecture as planes. The German Pavilion, Barcelona by Ludwig Mies van der Rohe.

Figure 4.26 . . .

The sloping plane of La Scala di Spagna, Rome.

ground plane. This design illustrates the power of the plane as a design tool, and also illustrates the potential of the plane to indicate direction, much like the line. The Red and Blue Chair by Gerrit Rietveld is a visually engaging exploration of the line and the plane in the design of a chair. Architect Ludwig Mies van der Rohe used planar elements for the design of the German Pavilion in 1923 at the Barcelona Exposition. He purposefully allowed the various planes to float free of one another so that they might be identified as purely planar elements. The ground plane can be sloped to create dramatic visual interest while being very functional such as has been done at the Scala di Spagna (Spanish Steps) in Rome. Curving planes have also been used throughout our history. Many contemporary designers are finding curving planes to be particularly interesting and appropriate for their design work.

Figure 4.27 . . .

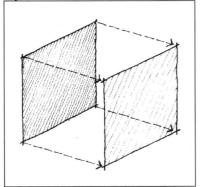

A plane moving through space forms a cube.

Figure 4.28 . . .

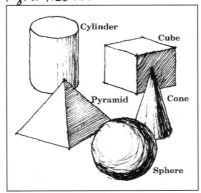

Illustrations of the Platonic Solids.

Figure 4.29 . . .

The Louvre Pyramid, Paris by I.M. Pei and Partners.

Figure 4.30 . . .

A spherical building, Le Geode, Paris by Andreas Fainsilber.

Figure 4.31 . . .

The implied cubic space of Place Vendome in Paris. Four walls and an implied roof plane at the top of the buildings.

Figure 4.32 . . .

An implied cylindrical space of a tunnel created by overhanging trees in Fargo.

## VOLUME

Volume involves the three dimensional world. The volumetric elements used by environmental designers have height, width and depth. Volume also has a place in space; volumes displace space and/or enclose space within them. We can conceive of a volume being created by moving a plane through space. Of course anything we show in this book is just an illusory two-dimensional representation of a volume. We can only show the likeness of volumes in two dimensional media such as drawing. The conventions of drawing three dimensional volumes is very important because as environmental designers we must communicate three dimensional ideas to other people. Sometime in the not-too-distant future we may be able to enter into and walk around virtual worlds that we create before they are built. This will certainly change the way we communicate design.

Our landscape is full of volumetric elements occurring naturally; rocks, conch shells, almost anything around us. As an environmental designer we use these natural volumetric elements, but we also create volumes as we alter the built environment for our own use. The most basic volumetric forms that we use are the platonic solids: the sphere, the cylinder, the cube, the cone, and the pyramid. The platonic solids are the building blocks of environmental design. Similar to lines and points, we can also use volumes as solid forms or as implied forms, as pure volumes or as altered forms. Although not often used as pure volumes in environmental design, there are examples of platonic solids used in an almost pure form. The entrance building at the Louvre in Paris is a crystal pyramid. The Geode, also in Paris, is as pure a sphere as you are likely to see in a built form. Many urban squares create a cubic volume with an implied top enclosure. In many towns in the mid-west we find tunnels of space created when the giant elm trees enclose the street with their canopies (see Figure 4.32).

Figure 4.33 . . .

A building in a classical (Greek Revival) style.

Figure 4.34 . . .

A more recent "modernist" space, the United Terminal at O'Hare International Airport by Murphy Jahn Architects.

Figure 4.35 . . .

A marker in the landscape illustrative of the deconstructivist style. Parc de la Villette, Paris by Bernard Tschumi.

## TIME

Although environmental designers work primarily in the third dimension, we must keep in mind that our work is strongly linked to time. Four separate and interrelated aspects of time impact environmental design. First, we create alterations to our built environment that are a product of their time. They are influenced by the current state of our culture, by the technology in place at the time, by the materials available, by the financing methods utilized and by the political climate. As much as we would like to create timeless designs, we will always be linked to our place in time. This aspect of time in environmental design also relates to the concept of style. Style is our way of identifying a shared direction in design at any given period of time. "It seems to me that style is one of the enduring—and endearing—aspects of architecture. Architects are being naïve in denying validity to the concept of style."[1] This quote from Witold Rybczynski hints at the power and the controversy of style in the environmental design fields. We may not like to be classified as practicing in a particular style but our place in time pretty much secures our work being categorized in a style. The illustrations above show buildings in three

[1]Rybczynski, Witold. (2001). *The Look of Architecture.* The Oxford University Press, New York. Page XIII.

different styles: Greek Revival, Modernism, and Deconstruction. As mentioned in Part 2 of this book, environmental designers seems to cycle through styles, always returning to the comfort of past accomplishments just prior to embarking on new stylistic directions, new expressions of time in our designs.

Second, the ravages of time are continually at work on our built environment. The materials that we use grow, age, change color and eventually deteriorate. Good environmental design improves with age. It matures and gains character. A landscape is the most identifiable example of this, but it is true of all types of environmental design. All environmental design must eventually be repaired, rebuilt or removed, as it ages beyond its effective life. The understanding of this aging process is critical to the long term success of design work.

Third, the built environment is affected minute by minute by the elements of the natural environment. The quality of the light changes constantly. We could be experiencing bright sunlight one minute and overcast skies the next. It might be dry or humid, smells are always present, we feel textures differently under different conditions. All of these environmental conditions affect the way that we perceive and react with the built environment. Great environmental designers utilize this passing of time to enliven their design work; to create mystery, intrigue, exposure and surprise.

The final aspect of time that impacts environmental design might be the most important for designers. We almost always experience environmental design as we move through the environment. We experience the built environment through time as we move from one place to another. We have a continually changing perspective of the pieces that make up our built environment. As environmental designers we must continually remind ourselves that we experience most of our spaces by moving. The Greek Temple complexes such as the Acropolis used this knowledge in a very effective way, as people arriving for a religious ceremony were led through continually changing views of the buildings and the landscape as they approached the temple. The changing views of the Acropolis, shown right, illustrate this concept. The use of the fourth dimension, time, is as important to an environmental designer as is the mastery of the elements of the other three dimensions.

*Figure 4.36 . . .*

The ancient Roman Wall in ruin in London.

*Figure 4.37 . . .*

Shadows and textures of aging materials.

*Figure 4.38 . . .*

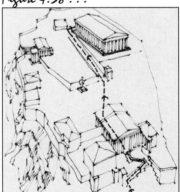

The unfolding of views over time at The Acropolis, Athens.

One challenge that time presents to environmental designers is the inescapably slow process of construction. It is often several years from the time that a designer conceives of a building, an interior or a landscape and the time that he or she can walk into that physical creation. The learning process for a designer is lengthened when you make a decision in year one of a project, but cannot evaluate the true success or failure of that decision until year three or four of the project. The first photograph in Part 4 of this book is of the Salt Lake City Library under construction. The following photograph was taken inside that library but two years later, shortly after it opened.

## Chapter 14 Sketch Activity

Spend some time wandering around your university looking for examples of the basic design elements in use. In your sketchbook do an individual sketch that illustrates each of the following basic design elements.

*Point*

*Line*

*Plane*

*Volume*

Figure 4.39 . . .

The public entry of the Salt Lake City Library by Moshe Sofdie.

# Chapter 15
# Perception and Design

Human beings have specific abilities to perceive the environment around them. Environmental designers must understand the human capacity for perception, and must develop their own capabilities to a high level. We will start the challenge of understanding perception with the introduction of the perceptual frame and the Gestalt principles of perception.

## PERCEPTUAL FRAME

All design work exists within a frame of reference. Painting often exists within a literal frame, pieces of wood or metal used to define the extent of the piece of artwork. Environmental design also has a frame of reference. We often call the frame for environmental design the "context." Even the point that we presented before has a frame

Figure 4.40 . . .

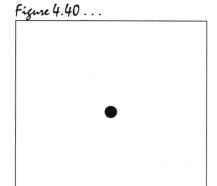

A point that is balanced and stable in its field.

Figure 4.41 . . .

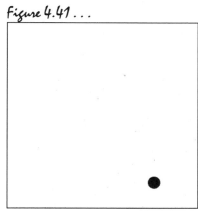

A point in tension and implying movement in its field.

Figure 4.42 . . .

London as the context for an environmental design project.

Figure 4.43 . . .

Fargo, North Dakota as context for an environmental design project.

Figure 4.44 . . .

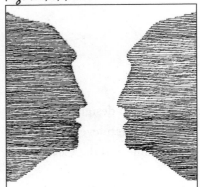

Which view is positive and which is negative?

Figure 4.45 . . .

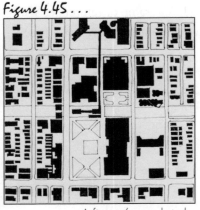

A figure/ground study.

of reference. It has a relationship to the paper on which it is drawn. That relationship has characteristics that we associate with balance or tension, stability or movement. In Figure 4.40 a point is shown in the center of its frame. Being equidistant from each edge of the frame, the point seems to be at rest. It seems to be stable and balanced in its field. Figure 4.41 shows that same point off center in the frame. There is a visual tension that is created between the point and the frames' edges that are close. Even without the illustration in Figure 4.40 we would feel that the point in Figure 4.41 has moved away from its point of balance. It has implied some movement within the frame. One of the contexts for urban design, landscape architecture and architecture is the city. Each city is different, demanding a different approach to environmental design.

The objects that we place in a frame of reference can be solid objects or implied objects. We often refer to this distinction as either positive or negative form. This is not an indication of value. Environmental designers determine which form to identify as positive or negative. Is Figure 4.44 a chalice or two faces? The figure/ground diagram uses the same principle to investigate the built nature of the city. It is often presented with all buildings being dark (as shown here) and again with buildings being left white, switching the positive and negative designation.

Consideration of the perceptual frame expands and strengthens the creative nature of environmental design. Our response to the context, our perceptual frame, is a primary factor in the success or failure of environmental design.

## PSYCHOLOGICAL PRINCIPLES OF PERCEPTION

Many psychologists have studied the ways that our senses and brains receive and process information. Gestalt psychologists were particularly interested in the ways that we receive and process visual information, and they reached some interesting conclusions that impact the ways that environmental designers work and communicate. These principles of perception appear to be genetically-based and not dependent on cultural influences.

Figure 4.46 . . .

Seeing step 1: Seeing and identifying repetitive cylinders and cones.

The primary principle of perception is our innate desire to spontaneously organize any sensory data that we receive. Human beings have a need to organize and classify the things around us; a need to understand what we see and to imbue it with meaning. We do this in a rather specific way, common to all people.

When we look at visual objects we first identify overall shape and pattern, and then we seek more detailed information. As we identify shapes and patterns, we seek to classify them, to match them with something that we already know. Looking at the left, we first identify the cylindrical shapes topped with cones. We recognize the repetition, or pattern of the form, and then we immediately want to place a meaningful name to this form, in this case "silos." In viewing the "Geode" by Adrien Fainsilber, we first identify the shape as a sphere by mentally closing the form. Our ability, some would say our compulsion, to seek closure in the objects around us, allows us to make sense of our visual world. The human tendency to seek closure of forms is very important and can be an important tool for environmental designers. Once we identify the sphere we begin to ask what it contains, what meaning does it have. Since we have no information appropriate to the use of a sphere, we have to be satisfied with our knowledge that it is indeed a sphere. By the way, it contains an Omni Theater and is located in Parc de la Villette in Paris. As a part of our initial pattern and shape recognition, we assign a relative size or scale to the forms we see. Is it big or small? We most often identify the size of an object relative to our own size. "Human scale" is a measurement we all can relate with.

*Figure 4.47 . . .*

We identify a sphere in this photo at Parc de la Villette.

*Figure 4.48 . . .*

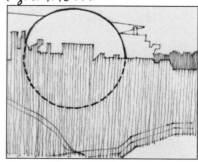

An illustration of how we visually close the sphere in order to identify it.

*Figure 4.49 . . .*

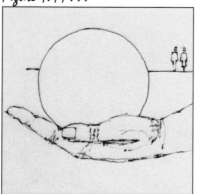

Scale: How big is the object? Is the sphere a building or a ball?

*Figure 4.50 . . .*

Seeing step 2: Focusing more to pick out larger details.

After we have established the overall pattern and shape of the object(s) in our view, we then start to look for more detailed information. We identify the repetitive pattern of triangular pieces that make up the whole of the Geode; we see the color and texture of the surface; we identify the vertical ribs in the silos, the pattern of the metal panels, the color and reflectivity of the surface, a sense of the hardness of the material and the effect of the sun on the surface.

*Figure 4.51 . . .*

Seeing step 3: Looking even closer
to see texture, structure, material
and color.

## Chapter 15 Sketch Activity

Do a sketch in your sketchbook that illustrates each of the following
perceptual ideas within design.

Sketch the exterior context of the classroom you are in for this course.

Do a sketch from the vicinity that illustrates the idea of visual completion of a
built form.

Do a series of sketches (3) that illustrate how we see an object in our
environment.

# Principles for Manipulating the Basic Design Elements

An understanding of human visual perception is the beginning of the very complex process of environmental design. The following section on design manipulation introduces the basic ways that we begin to create form in our environment. These principles apply to any design effort regardless of the design discipline. We will introduce the principles of form manipulation, the most common ordering principles used in design, and some of the proportioning systems used in environmental design.

## THE PRINCIPLES OF FORM MANIPULATION

Three dimensional forms and spaces are manipulated by using one of the following three principles: additive, subtractive, and transformation. The principle of additive form manipulation involves, as you might guess from the term, the combining of distinctive individual pieces into a larger whole. Subtractive form manipulation involves the cutting away or removal of portions of a whole form. Transformation of forms involves the pushing, pulling or twisting of the basic volumetric forms. Any given project created by an environmental designer might use a combination of these principles of form manipulation.

## ORDERING PRINCIPLES

As we begin to create forms and manipulate them with the principles introduced above, we also start to visually order the forms. We order multiple forms to create larger wholes and we order the constituent parts to create pleasing forms. These ordering principles are ways that we can respond to our human visual perception. Ordering principles are not present in every environmental design project, but they exist in a majority of successful designs.

Figure 4.52 . . .

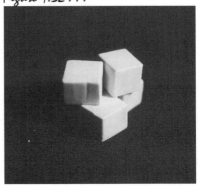

The ADDITIVE form of design manipulation.

Figure 4.53 . . .

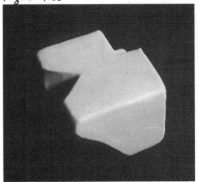

The SUBTRACTIVE form of design manipulation.

Figure 4.54 . . .

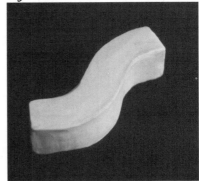

The TRANSFORMATIVE form of design manipulation.

Figure 4.55...

The ground plane as a DATUM for an urban square.

Figure 4.56...

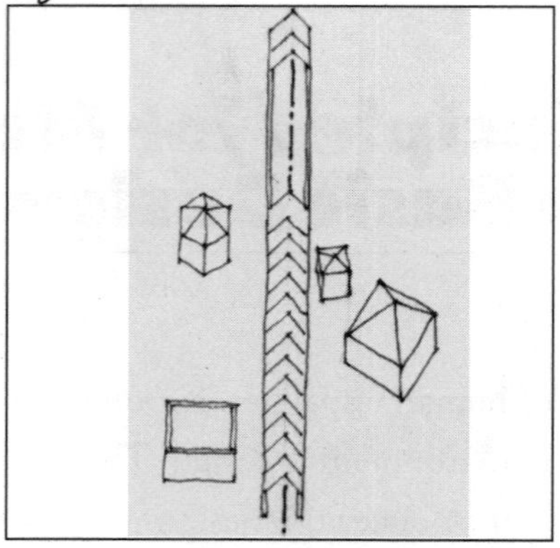

An axis, in this case a hallway, as a DATUM for a house by Cesar Pelli.

A DATUM gives a base to build on. It may be a strong podium as in the Greek Temples or a vertical organizing line or a horizontal axis in the landscape. The datum line in environmental design is something that is always easy to visually return to as a touchstone, a base for our observation.

Figure 4.57...

The BILATERAL SYMMETRY of the human form.

Balance is something that we all feel instinctively. Without it we would fall over when we walked. VISUAL BALANCE is much the same. Visual balance concerns the physical distribution of forms and the perceived weight of design forms. Balance has two components: SYMMETRICAL BALANCE and ASYMMETRICAL BALANCE. Symmetrical balance is defined by Webster's as "correspondence in size, shape and relative position of parts on opposite sides of a dividing line . . . a center or axis." Symmetry can be bilateral, as humans are, or radial. (See illustrations.) Asymmetric balance is not symmetric but balanced nonetheless, it is an informal balance. Asymmetric balance can be achieved using perceived weight of objects, color, texture, position and the attraction of the observer's eye.

Figure 4.58...

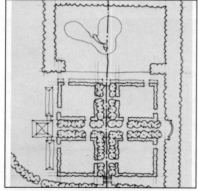

The BILATERAL SYMMETRY of the Minneapolis Sculpture Garden.

Figure 4.59...

RADIAL SYMMETRY of a tile pattern for a floor.

Figure 4.60...

An illustration of ASYMMETRICAL BALANCE. The composition is balanced left to right around the dark vertical inset. A thesis project by Mario Botta.

Figure 4.61...

An example of HIERARCHY. The dome at St. Paul's Cathedral in London is undoubtedly the most important part of the building. Sir Christopher Wren

Figure 4.62...

An illustration of REPETITION. An ossuary at the Cemetery of San Cataldo by Aldo Rossi.

Figure 4.63...

An illustration of RHYTHM at the Marin County Courthouse by Frank Lloyd Wright. There is a definite rhythmic pattern to the stacked arched openings in this building.

HIERARCHY places emphasis on a specific spot within the design. It often uses additive manipulation to establish a single spot or space that is more important than anywhere else in the composition. Size and shape of forms as well as color are also used to establish hierarchy in environmental design.

RHYTHM and REPETITION in environmental design have very close ties to our understanding of the concepts in music. The repetitious and rhythmic use of forms in environmental design is a very powerful, and potentially successful way, to manipulate designed space. Rhythm is closely allied with motion and time. The rhythms created might be "legato" or "staccato," they might be consistent or alternating, or progressive. Repetition and rhythm are easily and naturally recognized by humans and therefore have an important place in environmental design.

An ordering principle that has gained favor in the late 20th century is that of LAYERING. The principle involves placing one design idea on top of another, such as was done by Bernard Tschumi at Parc de la Villette in Paris. The design ideas layered in the park included a grid of follies, a rhythmic circulation path, axial water features and existing buildings. Each was organized on the site by its own system and then layered on top of one another.

Figure 4.64...

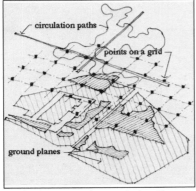

The layering of Parc de la Villette in Paris by Bernard Tschumi. Layers of circulation, points, and ground planes superimposed on top of each other.

Figure 4.65...

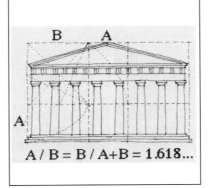

The Golden Section applied to a Greek Temple front. The Golden Section is a proportioning system developed by the ancient Greeks.

Figure 4.66...

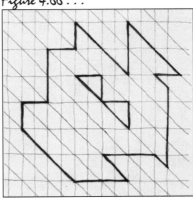

An example of a building perimeter generated by using field theory, a proportioning system developed by Walter Netsch of SOM.

PROPORTIONING SYSTEMS are formally established processes to help ensure ordered environmental designs. Most proportioning systems reinforce visual balance, so that we feel comfortable with the results. Proportioning systems are numerous and vary from the Golden Section developed by the ancient Greeks to mathematical ratios of depth, to length to width employed by Palladio in the Renaissance, to field theory developed by the American architect Walter Netsch. The details of these specific proportioning systems are covered extensively in other design literature and are therefore not dealt with in detail here.

## Chapter 16 Sketch Activity

Venture out into your city and find examples of the manipulation of basic design elements. Record in your sketchbook an example of each of the principles of manipulation and ordering.

*Additive*

*Subtractive*

*Tranformation*

*Datum*

*Bilateral Symmetry*

*Radial Symmetry*

*Assymetrical Balance*

*Hierarchy*

*Repetition*

*Rhythm*

# Spatial Relationships and Organization of Basic Design Elements

Environmental design, as we have talked about earlier in this book, is involved with the three dimensional world experienced in four dimensions. Our work is the design and manipulation of the space around us. We have introduced the methods of design manipulation which deal with abstract ideas applied to design. We will now look at the ways that can relate one space to another, and to organize them into meaningful wholes.

## SPATIAL RELATIONSHIPS BETWEEN BASIC DESIGN ELEMENTS

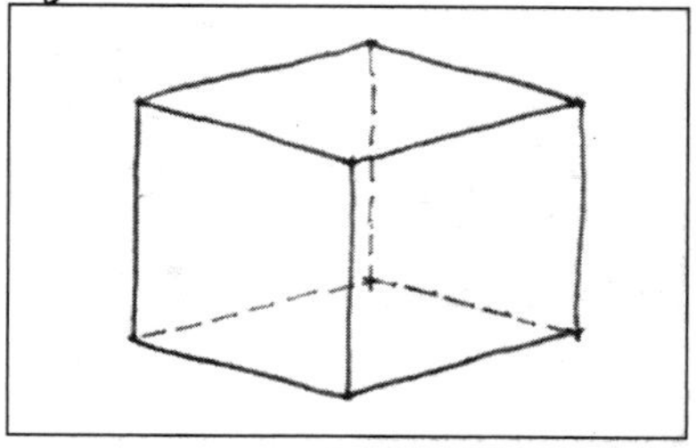

The ways that individual spaces relate to one another establish their spatial relationship. There are only five ways that spaces can relate to one another.

A SINGULAR SPACE stands alone without a relationship to any adjoining spaces. Its only relationship is to its context. This is literally an impossible situation, since a space in context must have some relationship to the spaces that make up its context. However, we think of a singular space as being without a relationship to any other primary space.

ADJACENT SPACES are just that; they are placed next to each other, therefore establishing a relationship. They do not touch each other and are not connected in any way. The distance between the two or more spaces establishes a degree of tension between the spaces. The closer to each other, without touching, the greater the tension created. The moment the two spaces touch, the visual tension between them vanishes.

Another spatial relationship involves spaces that are LINKED by a common space. Two or more spaces can be linked by a common space or a series of common spaces. Two rooms linked by a hallway is a familiar example. Two activity spaces in a park linked by a sidewalk would be a similar condition.

Figure 4.67 . . .

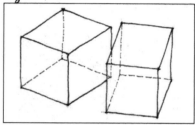

A SINGULAR space.

Figure 4.68 . . .

ADJACENT spaces.

Figure 4.69 . . .

An example of adjacent spaces (buildings) in Salt Lake City.

Figure 4.70...

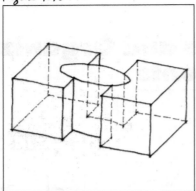

Spaced LINKED by a common space.

Figure 4.71...

An illustration of linked spaces at the East Gallery of the National Gallery of Art in Washington, D.C. by I.M. Pei.

The fourth spatial relationship is that of INTERLOCKING SPACES. Two or more spaces that intersect each other, sharing some space between them. The illustration shows two cubes interlocked together. The interlocking spaces can retain their individual identity; they can imply their individual identity; or they can loose their individual identity to the new whole. Frank Gehry, a prominent living architect uses interlocking spaces a great deal.

Figure 4.72...

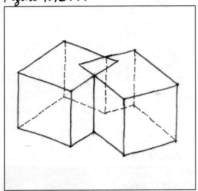

INTERLOCKING spaces.

The final spatial relationship is a SPACE WITHIN A SPACE. This is when one or more spaces are totally enclosed by another, larger space.

The illustrations of the spatial relationships show simplistic examples. In the designed world these relationships can become much more complex and harder to identify. The relationship of one space to another occurs in any direction—up, down, sideways. Built features in the environment might also employ several of the spatial relationships discussed above. Look around you to discover how the spaces that you walk through are linked to one another.

Figure 4.73...

An example of interlocking spaces in the Winton Guest House by Frank Gehry.

Figure 4.74...

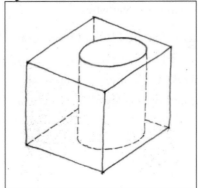

SPACE WITHIN A SPACE.

Figure 4.75...

St. Paul's Altar in London creates a space inside the domed space of the cathedral.

# STRATEGIES FOR SPATIAL ORGANIZATION

Spatial organization is distinctive from the spatial relationship of one space to another. Physical spaces are typically organized in one of five ways. These five spatial organization methods include: centralized, clustered, linear, radial, and grid. Built spaces usually exhibit at least one form of spatial relationship (as discussed in the last section) and one form of spatial organization as illustrated below. Building spaces, interiors, landscape spaces, even city spaces could utilize an interlocking relationship *and* be organized in a linear fashion.

CENTRALIZED spatial organization places spaces around a major central space or point. A good example of centralized organization is a cathedral such as St. Paul's Cathedral in London. All major spaces in the building are arranged around the central domed space.

A CLUSTERED organization is similar to a centralized one, but a single space does not act as the center. In a clustered organization there may be many centers (important spaces) or no centers. Clustering seems to be a more naturalistic way of organizing design elements. It is used extensively in Landscape Architecture when the designer wants to have designed spaces look natural. For other environmental designers, clustering provides a more haphazard, less formal look to their compositions.

A form of spatial organization that many of us are familiar with is LINEAR organization. Many of our public buildings, interiors and landscape spaces are organized along a line. The line used to organize these spaces is most often a form of circulation, such as a sidewalk or a hall, although linear organization does not always use circulation as its line. The organizing line can have all of the characteristics of the line that we introduced earlier in this book. Linear organization is a very effective way to relate functional spaces to one another, but it can be a particularly boring way to organize spaces.

*Figure 4.76 . . .*

CENTRALIZED organization.

*Figure 4.77 . . .*

The centralized organization of a building at the State of Illinois Building in Chicago. All rooms are organized around the central atrium space.

*Figure 4.78 . . .*

CLUSTERED Organization.

*Figure 4.79 . . .*

A cluster of trees on the North Dakota State University campus.

*Figure 4.80 . . .*

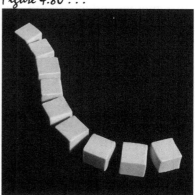

LINEAR Organization.

Figure 4.81 . . .

The linear organization of an interior space. The connector tunnel between concourses at the United Terminal at O'Hare International Airport, Chicago by Murphy Jahn.

Figure 4.82 . . .

RADIAL organization.

Figure 4.83 . . .

GRIDiron organization.

Figure 4.84 . . .

The grid of streets of Salt Lake City at night.

Related to linear organization is RADIAL organization. Spaces that are organized in a form that radiates from a central point. The distinction between a centralized organization and a radial organization is that a radial form does not center on the point or origin, but moves out from that point.

The GRID is a form of spatial organization that is used extensively in cities in the United States. It is an efficient and practical way to organize many built forms. A gridiron organization can utilize any network of lines, regular or irregular, to establish the location of built spaces. The most common gridiron organization is a regular, rectangular grid. However, designers occasionally use other grids such as the triangular grid used by I.M. Pei in the planning and structure for the East Gallery of the National Gallery of Art. The United States is dominated by the grid. Our property ownership, for much of the country, is tied to the national grid of one mile by one mile, which creates sections of land that can be easily measured and recorded.

Each of these spatial organization methods can be used in any direction. We can organize vertically such as in a high rise building, or we can organize horizontally such as in a park. Environmental design projects are a complex, three dimensional assemblage of spaces related to one another, and organized in some fashion. Study your surroundings and identify the relationships and organizations that you see in use.

# Chapter 17 Sketch Activity

Spend some time exploring the buildings on your university campus as well as the landscape spaces of the campus. Identify and sketch examples of each of the following spatial relationships and spatial organizations.

*Singular space*

*Adjacent spaces*

*Spaces linked by a common space*

*Interlocking spaces*

*A space within a space*

*Centralized organization*

*Clustered organization*

*Linear organization*

*Radial organization*

*Gridiron organization*

# PART 5

# Ponderables

*I* would now like to explore some of the ideas and concepts that keep environmental designers up late at night. I call these issues and concepts ponderables. These ponderables vex us at times and excite us at other times. They are always a part of our lives, but are very difficult to define and even harder to justify in quantifiable terms. I have chosen to organize these ponderables in three pairs of issues. *Beauty* and *quality* are discussed in Chapter 18, *value* and *economics* in Chapter 19 and *creativity* and *collaboration* in Chapter 20.

Environmental design faces tremendous challenges to convince clients and the public that what we do is worthwhile and contributes to the betterment of everyone's lives. Other professions do not face similar challenges to their validity. Doctors, lawyers and engineers work in pretty absolute conditions. When any one of them approaches a problem, they look for specific solutions that are either right or wrong. If they are right, as we expect them to be, then they are successful. If they are wrong often enough, we make sure that they cannot continue to practice their profession. Their solution worked or it didn't. Successful environmental design is more than just providing something that works. Successful environmental design must not only work, but it should be elegant and be an inspiration for people. Lifting the spirits of people as they go about their daily lives is not only hard to do but almost impossible to measure.

# Chapter 18
# Beauty and Quality

An area that vexes all environmental designers is the question of beauty. Just what is beauty? How do we determine what is beautiful? And, who decides what is beautiful? It just seems so unfair that people, untrained in the fields of environmental design, decide whether our work is beautiful or not. Why is it even important that environmental design work be beautiful?

As mentioned earlier, several centuries ago Marcus Vitruvius Polio, writing about architecture, postulated that for architecture to be successful, of high quality, and true it must contain three qualities. It must possess comitas, firmitas and venustas.[1] Many years later an Englishman Sir Henry Wotton translated these terms to mean commodity, firmness, and delight. As we think about these terms related to architecture, and indeed to the broader field of environmental design, they provide for us a way to begin to evaluate environmental design projects.

If an environmental design project is to be considered of high quality using Vitruvius' scale, then the project must solve the problem at hand well and for a reasonable expense. We would consider these characteristics to represent the commodity of the project. Does the office building house workers in a way that enables them to complete their work easily and efficiently? Does the building protect their health, safety and welfare and do so at a reasonable cost to the owners and society? Does the park provide facilities for the activities desired and does it contribute to the sustainability of the natural environmental systems?

If the project is built with materials and techniques that will stand the test of time, then the project may be considered to have good firmness. Firmness for the park might include evaluation of how the trees and plants in the park grow and enhance the environment. How the maturing park can be responsive to changing needs of the people that use the park. Firmness for the building involves the ability to be strong and viable for a long period of time. This should include the ability for the building to outlast the original purpose for which it was built. Renovation of buildings into new uses is a great example of firmness. The office in which I am writing this book (see Figure 5.1) is in its third life as a building. The building was originally built to house an agricultural implement and supply dealership. Years later it was converted to a school supply store and warehouse and in 2004 was converted into the North Dakota State University Downtown Campus, which houses the art, architecture and landscape architecture programs of the university.

Figure 5.1 . . .

NDSU Downtown in Fargo, North Dakota. The building, built in 1903, now houses the art, architecture and landscape architecture programs of North Dakota State University.

[1]Kostof, Spiro. (1995). *A History of Architecture: Settings and Rituals.* Oxford University Press, New York, Page 13.

Figure 5.2 . . .

An architecture studio in the renovated
NDSU Downtown building.

Figure 5.3 . . .

A more recent example of an agricultural implement dealership in
Fargo, North Dakota.

Although this building was built in 1903 as an implement dealership, the quality of the materials used in its construction, and the design that was employed, have made the building very valuable as other, vastly different uses have been incorporated into the building. The amount and quality of light from the large windows made it easy to find and sell the agricultural implements stored in the building and today, it also is tremendous for studio spaces for artists and designers. I am afraid that the buildings that we are building currently as implement dealerships do not have the same degree of firmness contained in the NDSU Downtown building (see Figure 5.3).

The third quality prized by Vitruvius was that of venustas, or delight. This is where the notion of beauty comes into the discussion of the quality of environmental design projects. Delight implies that there is a positive emotional response to the building, landscape or interior with which we are engaged. I also think that the term beauty indicates the same types of qualities that Vitruvius was trying to define. Beauty has been lost in today's culture of complaint. As an example, type beauty into a search engine on the internet and the first page of results is about beauty aids or pornography. We seem to have lost any shared sense of what it means for something to be beautiful. Let's start by looking at a couple of dictionary definitions of beauty and delight.

> **Beauty**—1: the quality or aggregate of qualities in a person or thing that gives pleasure to the senses or pleasurably exalts the mind or spirit: loveliness
> 3: a particularly graceful, ornamental, or excellent quality[2]

> **Beauty**—a combination of qualities that give pleasure to the sight or other senses or to the mind.[3]

> **Beautiful**—1: having qualities of beauty; exciting aesthetic pleasure
> 2: generally pleasing; excellent, beautiful applies to whatever excites the keenest of pleasure to the senses and stirs emotion through the senses. Handsome suggests aesthetic pleasure due to proportion, symmetry, or elegance (a handsome Georgian mansion) (see footnote 1)

> **Delight**—1: to please greatly. 2. To be greatly pleased, to feel great pleasure.[4]

[2]Mish, Frederick C. (1993). *Merriam-Webster's Collegiate Dictionary, Tenth Edition*. Merriam-Webster, Inc., Springfield, MA.
[3]Ehrlich, E., Flexner, S.B., Carruth, G., & Hawkins, J.M. (1980). *Oxford American Dictionary*. New York: Avon Books. Page 53.
[4]Ibid, Page 168.

It is clear from these definitions that if we are to meet the qualities set forth by Vitruvius, we must design in such a way as to touch the emotions of people. Terms such as "pleasurably exalts the mind or spirit" indicate a very high level of expectations in order for our projects to be delightful and beautiful. I am afraid that many designers have lost track of beauty and delight as serious goals for their work. Our society has contributed to this problem as we seek to create an egalitarian society where everyone is of value and no idea or opinion is better than another. Society often gives up the quest for beauty, delight and excellence in everything that we do. In environmental design we cannot afford to give up on excellence or on beauty.

Two other trends in our society seem to be in contrast to our abandonment of excellence, delight and beauty. Our fascination with "the beautiful people" of our world baffles me. The amount of credence that we give to the opinions of movie stars and athletes are of great concern. Why would the opinion of a movie star about the beauty and functionality of a particular product have any more validity than your opinion or mine? We should dismiss "the beautiful people" as an arbiter of what is beautiful and valuable. The other trend that seems to be happening is a perceptual raising of the value of design in many aspects of our lives. The design and quality of some household goods has been improving, as mass marketers such as Target begin to hire designers to create products. Design seems to be a more important topic for a larger number of people than ever before.

Some of the research that my firm has conducted over the years supports this notion that public opinion about design is improving and that it has always been much better than we might have realized. Our urban design and planning work has often required us to solicit the opinions and preferences of the public as we design their future neighborhoods or towns. To establish a set of shared values for the community, we have used a visual preference survey, asking people to look at pairs of photographs and to choose their favorite. We have been looking for preferences in planning, such as where to put commercial buildings and parking; in architecture, such as what an entryway ought to look like, or what housing style is preferred; in landscapes, such as the qualities of a street or park. Some of our findings follow.

Figure 5.4 . . .

Historical Interiors: The Rookery Building in Chicago and the Hall of Battles at Versailles.

Figure 5.5...

Library Interiors: The city library entrance in Salt Lake City and in Minneapolis.

Figure 5.6...

Circulation stairs in the Minneapolis Institute of Art in Minneapolis and the deYoung Museum in San Francisco.

Figure 5.7...

Major display spaces in the Utah Museum of Fine Arts in Salt Lake City and the deYoung Museum in San Francisco.

In each of these pairs of photographs the image on the left was preferred by a substantial margin over the photograph to the right. (The order of their presentation was mixed during the survey and all of the photographs used were in color.) The preferences were in the 60 to 80% range. After questioning the respondents about what qualities contributed to their preference, the overwhelming response was the amount of natural light. Secondarily, many people mentioned the warmth or coolness of the colors as contributing to their opinion. The preference was for warmer colors. Each of these spaces are good spaces. Each is well designed utilizing excellent materials and superior workmanship. One in each pair seems to be preferred. One in each pair seems to strike an emotional cord with people.

When we looked at housing types and styles we found some rather interesting results. When shown the following pair of photographs the preference was for the more traditional house shown on the right. However, the preference was not as strong as we thought it might be. The traditional home was preferred by about 10% more of the respondents than the modern home.

Villa Savoy in Poissy, France and a more traditional home in Fargo, North Dakota.

The ubiquitous apartment building, which is common throughout the United States, is never preferred over any other type of housing. Shown below is an apartment building compared with a series of town homes. The town home, even within suburban communities, is preferred by greater than 80% of the respondents.

An apartment building and a town home development.

One might ask then why our builders continue to construct apartment buildings similar to the one shown? When the market tends to offer only this one choice to tenants there really is no choice. Other preferences we have discovered also beg similar questions. In survey after survey the public shows a preference for housing that has clear, distinct entries on the front of the house leading to a public sidewalk. In each pair of photographs presented below the survey respondents preferred the image on the left.

Figure 5.10 . . .

A front versus side entry.

Figure 5.11 . . .

A clear entry and public sidewalk versus garages at the front.

Figure 5.12 . . .

A traditional housing development versus one with no public sidewalk.

A clear public front with a gracious entry is valued highly by the public. The preference rate has been as high as 90% in some of our surveys. Why is it that we continue to build projects like that shown in Figure 5.11 with nothing fronting the street except a garage? These homes were constructed in 2006. This preference for a clear public entry applies to commercial structures as well as housing.

The preference for public sidewalks leads us to consider some additional urban design and landscape characteristics. One of the issues confronting city planners and urban designers is whether to allow the development of strip retail centers in our cities? The argument from developers is typically that people want to park in front of stores so they have easy access. The same arguments are made by the retailers themselves. Our surveys would seem to indicate something else. In the two examples shown below, two of many, the survey respondents preferred stores located on the sidewalk over stores with parking provided in front of them by at least 70%.

Figure 5.13 . . .

Retail choices in Minneapolis/St Paul.

Figure 5.14 . . .

Retail choices in Minneapolis/St. Paul.

Preferences for more pleasing retail environments devoid of the automobile should direct our environmental design work. The automobile does not add to the quality or beauty of our environment. The results from the following set of choices presented to the public was not very surprising. The public preferred the tree covered street on the right by 95% over the street on the left.

Figure 5.15 . . .

Two collector streets in Fargo, North Dakota.

Both streets are classified the same way, as collector streets. The street design on the left has been driven almost exclusively by the needs of the automobile and does not consider the quality of the environment for all of the citizens. The street does have a sidewalk and street trees have been planted but it is clear that in 50 years when the landscape matures, it will still not be as pleasant as the street on the right. Although both streets accommodate the automobile and the pedestrian, it is clear which street feels better. Which street is more delightful to use?

It is my contention that the public is more attuned to beauty and quality in their surroundings than we typically give them credit for. Often, if we ask, we find a very real preference for those things that delight and help us to feel good over those things that are just mundane and add nothing of substance to the milieu. The identification of those design elements that make these positive contributions is not an easy task. It is a task that environmental designers should relish and pursue with great vigor. Ask your friends and family what it is that they like. Better yet, ask them why it is that they like the things that they like. Environmental designers need to train themselves to look below the surface expectations and dig out those things that really do matter to people.

*Beauty is not only in the eye of the beholder!!!* Beauty must first be in the eye of the person creating the things and places that are to be beheld by other people. Environmental designers have a responsibility to the society and the environment to educate ourselves. It is absolutely essential that we develop critical attitudes about our work. That we educate ourselves to understand what is beautiful and what is not; what constitutes good design and what does not. All design is not equal, some ideas are better than others.

## PROPORTIONING SYSTEMS AND BEAUTY

Proportioning systems have always been important to art, music and design. In her book *Divine Proportion*, Priya Hemenway discusses the relationship of our proportioning systems, particularly the divine proportion with the relationship to the human body. "Heraclitus (540–480 BCE), one of the most significant mystics of ancient Greece, once said, 'Man is the measure of all things.' Man or woman, we are the very balancing of the Divine Proportion. We are represented by the segment on Euclid's wonderful line that is proportionate to the whole in the same way it is to the balance of the line, and whatever we describe is a reflection of our relationship to the whole. Blessed with an innate sense of this proportion, our highest expression becomes art. When we deny the feeling of proportion within ourselves, we produce nothing of enduring significance."[5] This may be a bit strongly stated for us today, but it touches on something that I have felt for most of my thirty years as a designer: we have an innate sense of proportion, something that we are born with, we don't seem to have to learn it. Understanding proportion, particularly the divine proportion reinforces what we seem to have as an innate ability. It allows us to more easily use the strength of the divine proportion in our work. Divine proportion is both a mathematical ratio and a physical construct. The divine proportion is illustrated in Figure 5.16.

Figure 5.16 . . .

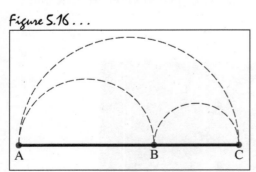

An illustration of a line divided into segments illustrating the divine proportion.

The line is divided into segments of divine proportion when the relationship between the whole line AC and the larger segment of line AB is the same as the relationship between the larger segment AB and the smaller segment of line BC. As a mathematical phrase this relationship would be expressed as AC/AB = AB/BC which we would

[5]Hemenway, Priya. (2005). *Divine Proportions*. Sterling Publishing: New York. Page 92.

read as AC is to AB as AB is to BC. This ratio is mathematically resolved to give us a ratio of approximately 1.61803 to 1. This ratio is referred to as the Divine Proportion, the Golden Mean, the Golden Proportion, the Golden Ratio, or the Golden Section. The Greeks referred to this ratio with the Greek letter Ø (Phi). The divine proportion can be found in both nature and in our built world. The pentagram, as illustrated in Figure 5.17 shows that the component lines of the pentagram increase in length at a ratio of 1.61803 from segment a to segment d.

Figure 5.17 . . .

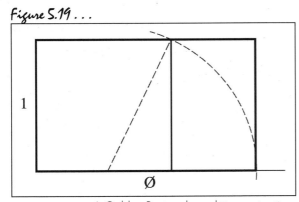

A pentagram based on the divine proportion.

Figure 5.18 . . .

The natural pentagram in the alignment of seeds in the center of an apple.

The Greeks used the Golden Rectangle as a proportioning tool for many of their most important buildings such as the temple buildings on the Acropolis. The Golden Rectangle has the dimension of 1 in one direction and Ø in the perpendicular direction. Figure 5.19 shows a Golden Rectangle and its construction. To construct the Golden Rectangle start with a square. Locate the center of the base segment of the square. Using that center point as the center of an arc draw an arc from one of the top corners of the square down, until it intersects with an extension of the base line of the square. From that intersection point, draw a vertical line perpendicular to the base and complete the rectangle.

We can also construct a Golden Spiral based on a nesting of Golden Rectangles. See Figure 5.21 for an illustration of this Golden Spiral. We see the Golden Spiral in the Nautilus Shell where the spiral of the shell is a

Figure 5.19 . . .

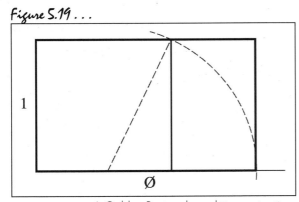

A Golden Rectangle and its construction.

Figure 5.20 . .

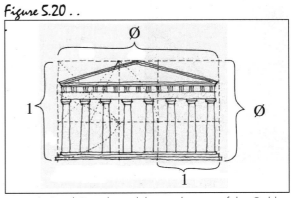

A Greek Temple and the application of the Golden Rectangle in its design.

Figure 5.21 . . .

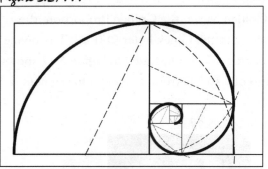

A Golden Spiral created by nesting Golden Sections together.

Figure 5.22 . . .

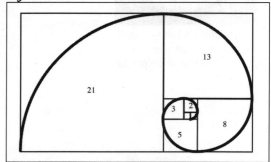

A Golden Rectangle constructed using squares with sides the length of the Fibonacci Sequence.

Figure 5.23 . . .

The spiral construction of a pineapple.

Golden Spiral, but the size of the chambers created as the mollusk grows increased in volume at a ratio approximating the Divine Proportion.

In the 12th century an Italian mathematician, Leonardo of Pisa discovered the unique characteristics of a sequence of numbers. His work was supposedly the result of a theoretical investigation into propagating rabbits. The sequence of numbers was 1, 1, 2, 3, 5, 8, 13, 21, 34, 55, . . . After his death, Leonardo of Pisa was given the nickname Fibonacci and the sequence has been known as the Fibonacci Sequence since. The sequence is unique because each successive number in the sequence is the result of adding the previous two numbers in the sequence. I mention this here in this discussion of the Divine Proportion because if we look at the ratio between numbers in the Fibonacci Sequence the ratio approaches the Divine Proportion, particularly as the numbers get larger. We can also approximate the Golden Rectangle by nesting squares with their sides the length of Fibonacci numbers as shown in figure 5.22. The rectangle created gets closer and closer to a true Golden Rectangle as the Fibonacci numbers increase.

The Fibonacci Sequence also shows up in other natural places such as the spiral construction of the pineapple and the layout of seeds in a sunflower. If you count the number of rows of seeds in the sunflower head that spiral in a clockwise direction, and then count the number in the counterclockwise direction they will differ and they will be adjacent numbers within the Fibonacci Sequence. Which means that their ratio to each other approaches the Divine Proportion.

In Part 4 of this book we looked at a few of the proportioning systems that have been used in environmental design over the years. Most of these are related in some way to the Divine Proportion discussed here. In Part 4 I wanted to look at some specific tools for using proportion, here I wanted to open us to the wonder of proportional systems so we can search for new ways to use them. I delve into this discussion because environmental designers, scientists, mathematicians, and others keep discovering links to the Divine Proportion. There is something to this notion that proportion is linked to the world around us. The more we understand about this and the more we understand the strength of proportion in our design work, the more opportunities we will have to complete quality work that has a chance to stand the test of time. Beauty is something all around us that we need to be able to tap into.

# Chapter 19

# Value and Economics

Value and economics make it possible for environmental designers to work. What we do is to provide a service for people. Environmental designers don't actually build anything. They determine needs and wishes, design a solution, oversee the construction and do all of that within an agreed upon range of costs. The clients of environmental designers must believe that the service that we provide has real value for them. The ability to provide both value and cost control are critical to our success or failure in environmental design.

**VALUE:** 1; a fair return or equivalent in goods, services, or money for something exchanged   2; the monetary worth of something   3; relative worth, utility, or importance   6a; relative lightness or darkness of a color: luminosity   b; the relation of one part in a picture to another with respect to lightness and darkness.[6]

The value that environmental designers bring to their projects is based on the knowledge and experience they have acquired throughout their careers. The ways that environmental designers might bring value to a building project include:

- A design that includes durable materials that are sustainable, will last for a very long time and are ultimately recyclable into other projects.

- Creating a project that will save the owner energy and other long-term costs.

- A project that will not pollute but will help clean the environment.

- Designing a project that is more desirable to renters or tenants. A project that attracts people that will support the businesses or activities.

- A design that is pleasing to users and neighbors alike.

- A design that encourages connections between people with social and work related benefits.

- Expertise in guiding a project through the codes, rules, and regulations of government.

- A design that helps people feel and be secure.

- Creating healthy, non-toxic environments.

- A design that fosters healing, learning, creativity or activity.

This is certainly not an exhaustive list of the values that an environmental designer might bring to a project for their clients. Value also resides in the design process itself which allows the designers to work very closely with their clients. The design process helps designers, users, and clients discuss the best possible outcomes for everyone involved. The collaboration between clients and a team of designers provides opportunities to focus on real value. Real value in environmental design includes function, durability, cost effectiveness, aesthetics and fit within

[6]Mish, Frederick C. (1993). *Merriam-Webster's Collegiate Dictionary, Tenth Edition*. Merriam-Webster, Inc. Springfield, MA.

nature. When one area of a project begins to dominate the design, it is up to the environmental design team to bring every aspect of the project back into balance. Sometimes conflicts arise between the owner's goals and the social and ecological goals that a designer is also bound to maintain. It is a part of the environmental designer's job to be the mediator and arrive at some consensus as projects move ahead.

Some members of the public have not always acknowledged the value that environmental designers bring to building projects. Some people look at a building, an interior or a garden and say "I can do that. I don't need to pay a professional to design that." If all someone wants in a garden is a pretty flower to bloom sometime in the summer then, indeed, anyone could do that. If what is wanted involves flowers blooming throughout the summer season, help in controlling insects or pests, draining rain water away from the foundation of the building and into the ground water, elimination of pollution in the ground water, and shading of the house to reduce summer cooling costs, then the services of a landscape architect are of great value.

The deplorable condition of our natural environment and the complexity of our cities and buildings increases significantly the importance of the work done by environmental designers. Environmental designers can bring value to every building project, large or small.

## THE INCREASED VALUE OF DESIGN

Simple functioning and elegant design of our consumer goods is becoming a broadly held expectation. Using Apple as an example: the iPod is very simple to use with elegant design and increasingly sophisticated functioning without increased complexity of operation. The simplicity of downloading music, movies, and podcasts from a huge library of possibilities, into a device that is incredibly easy to take along with you, doesn't skip and delivers incredible sound quality makes the iPod an incredible success. Even though it is an expensive technology, the combination of beauty, functionality and durability make it a product of value.

Steve Jobs believes that design is as important to the success of Apple products as is function and reliability. (Comitas, Firmitas, Venustas.) One of my favorite examples of a simple and elegant product was the introduction of the audio-video remote controller for Apple computers. In 2006 Steve Jobs introduced the new audio-video controller by first showing the remote controller offered by Microsoft. The Microsoft controller was approximately two inches wide, six inches long and about 3/4 of an inch thick with many different buttons. The new Apple remote controller was 1-1/4" wide, 3-1/4" long and 1/4" thick with two buttons. The Apple device controls the same functions in a much simpler and more elegant product. The resurgence of Apple Computer is in part due to their attention to design.

## THE BUSINESS OF DESIGN

Environmental design is a noble profession but it is also needs to be a business. The environmental design fields provide a livelihood for thousands of people worldwide. The majority of environmental designers work in small consulting firms that do a wide variety of work. These small firms have between 1 and 25 people in each firm and are located in cities around the world. Environmental design firms with more than 100 people are considered large firms. These large firms tend to have multiple environmental design disciplines within them. They do much more of the work within their own firms.

In addition to working in consulting design firms, environmental designers also work for corporations and government agencies. The design positions in corporations and agencies are very important and offer great opportunities for the environmental designers. The designers in these situations do not have the same set of business challenges that private consulting firms have, although they may have their own set of bureaucratic challenges.

The economic driver for environmental design firms is projects. Firms must have a continuous supply of projects to keep their employees busy and productive. Competition between firms is fierce for the available work. This competition ebbs and flows with the general economy. When the economy is good more clients are building projects. When the economy is bad, clients quit building. This fluctuation in the amount of work available has led design firms to look further afield for projects. With the advances in technology and communication even small firms located in remote cities are able to do design work anywhere in the world. Even though the competition for work is fierce, the design fields have a very interesting camaraderie between design firms. A great deal of work is accomplished by creating joint ventures of multiple environmental design firms. Short term partnerships between architects, landscape architects, interior designers, etc. are made to form a team with specific skills and experiences that would be applicable to the project being sought.

Whether an environmental design firm is seeking work as a part of a team or as an individual firm, the primary way for firms to acquire projects is to respond to "requests for proposals" (RFP). An owner will publish an RFP that outlines the required characteristics of the project they wish to undertake. The project characteristics might include any or all of the following:

- Type of occupancy and area of space required
- Activities required within the space or landscape
- Project budget
- Philosophy of the owners
- Specific design characteristics of the firm and its approach to their work
- Preferred color and material palettes
- Quality of light and views desired
- Relationships between people and activities
- Density of uses and mix of uses or types
- Commitment of owner to sustainability
- Expectations for the time of completion
- Relationship to the public
- Working processes employed
- Types and qualities of human interactions desired

The description of the project may be quite a bit more specific or it may include only the first three items above. The RFP will also ask the interested firms to provide information about their firm and their capability to complete the work in a creative, timely and effective way. Owners typically want to know who is going to work on their project, and what the roles of the various people will be. Owners may also ask for an indication of a range of fees that will be required to complete the project. The entire RFP process is based on selecting the most qualified environmental design firm to do the work. It is a process that helps the owner find the best fit for their needs. The working relationship between the design team and the owner's team is really critical to the success of the design project. Design projects are filled with emotion, personal desire, economic and technical constraints, and a great deal of communication. It is easy to have conflicts between various members of the design team. The real test is in how the team handles the inevitable conflicts on their way to the best possible solution for the project.

The publicly held perception is that environmental design professionals "bid" for their work. We often get asked if we are going to bid for a project. Bidding is a process where a company is asked to supply a particular product or service, of a set quality, for the least price possible. Many government agencies are mandated to competitively bid their building, interior design, or landscape construction projects and must accept the least expensive bid that meets the project requirements. Although this process is widely used in construction and product acquisition, it has some drawbacks and it is not appropriate for hiring professional services. When hiring a professional to do environmental design services, or any other service for that matter, cost is important but the experience of the firm and their ability to work with the client are much more important. For that reason environmental design firms are chosen on a qualifications basis not by lowest cost.

There are three other ways that environmental design firms obtain work. The first, and easiest, is to get work directly from clients through personal relationships or because the firm has done work for the owner in the past and it was successful. The relationships built with individuals and with companies can be very satisfying. They can be good for business as well. It is very satisfying both professionally and personally to be able to do repeat work for a client.

Environmental design firms may also enter design competitions to get large projects. Design competitions are a very interesting way for young firms to show that they can do extremely creative work. Design competitions are held throughout the world and take two main forms. The limited design competitions invite a select list of environmental design firms to participate. The invited firms are paid a nominal fee to prepare their submission to the competition. These competitions usually involve more well-known environmental design firms and are used by the owners to generate international interest in their project. The winners of the competition usually receive a contract to complete the project. An example of a competition where this did not happen was the international competition for the re-design of the World Trade Center in New York City after the buildings were destroyed in a terrorist attack. The winner of the international design competition was a beautifully sculpted building by Daniel Libeskind. The ensuing arguments and fighting about who actually owned the building site and had the right to develop the new projects ended with the firm of Skidmore, Owings and Merrill becoming the designers of the newly named "Freedom Tower" with Daniel Libeskind as a consultant to SOM.

Open design competitions invite participation from any registered design professional in the world. These design competitions pay nothing upfront to the participants, but do award prize money and the opportunity to negotiate to actually design the entire project. These competitions are a way for an owner to seek a number of great ideas for their project, and it gives younger, less well-known, design firms a chance to make their mark. There are always several major design competitions ongoing throughout the world. The various government entities in Great Britain have used the design competition a lot to seek excellent design for public buildings. A variation on the open design competition process is the "ideas" competition where a competition sponsor is looking for design ideas or publicity for a particular design-related cause. The winner of an ideas competition typically does not receive any award money or a commission, but may receive a great deal of publicity and media attention. I have very mixed feelings about the value of ideas competitions for the designers. The attention they might bring to an issue can have significant effect, but the value to the design firm is a bit questionable. My comments here are certainly biased and slanted by my own experiences. Any firm wishing to participate in an ideas competition must do so with a clear set of expectations and a desire to do good design work for society. Design competitions are not a really significant path to obtaining work, but they are fun to do and give firms opportunities to explore new ideas and to stretch their design wings. Some firms enter competitions regularly for just that reason. They want to keep fresh and inventive.

The third way to get work is for environmental design firms to become developers. Quite a number of environmental design firms have become the owners of the projects that they design. They have seen an opportunity to create a building, a store, a commercial landscape, or a large piece of the city and initiated the project themselves. This has become a much more common way for firms to keep busy; they develop projects themselves. This way of creating work carries with it an increased level of financial risk, but also includes an increased potential for financial gain.

## MAKING MONEY IN ENVIRONMENTAL DESIGN

Environmental design is like any other business. You must bring more money into the firm than you spend if you want to stay in business. This is a pretty easy concept to understand. The complexity of building projects and the increased expectations placed on environmental designers has made the process of environmental design more and more expensive over the years. The amount of very sophisticated equipment being used in the field has increased dramatically, but the largest increase in costs has occurred in the human capital of the profession. As projects become more complex we need more knowledge and more varied knowledge which requires more people to be involved in the projects. Increasingly, environmental designers are charged with a broader definition of health, safety and welfare which includes how we treat the planet and make it habitable for future generations. Sustainability is now a standard expectation in environmental design. A standard we must keep pushing and expanding.

Environmental design is a people-intensive profession like education or law. The major costs of doing the work are spent on the people that do the work. Close to 80% of the costs of a typical environmental design firm are in the people that work in the firm. The expenses associated with people, salary, taxes, insurance, etc. are not any different than most places of employment, but the work that we do cannot be automated or streamlined and robotized. It is complex, "wicked" work that requires many talented and highly educated people.

The ability of environmental design firms to make money is partly predicated on keeping a steady stream of work in the office. Factors such as economic cycles or supply shortages tend to complicate a firm's ability to maintain that steady flow of work. This is harder for a single discipline firm than it might be for a multi-discipline firm. For this reason, even relatively small firms often employ design professionals from several of the environmental design fields. In addition, concentration on a particular type of design work makes it harder to maintain a steady flow of work. As an example, if a firm concentrates on school buildings and the number of projects declines because of a funding change within a state legislature, it will be difficult for that firm to keep enough work in the office to justify their employees. If the firm is experienced in a wider variety of project types, then they will be better able to shift their emphasis when the work flow around them changes. For this reason, most environmental design firms are considered general practices.

All of the environmental design fields can provide very lucrative careers. Owners, who by law, typically have to be licensed, can be paid very well as they build value in the firm over the years. The value that they help create within the firm will become a return on their investment when they sell their share of the firm or their stock in the firm upon their retirement.

Environmental design is indeed a business. Many successful environmental design firms have a common set of characteristics in their ownership team. The firms have at least one partner that is a great designer. This lead designer sets the standards for all of the designers in the firm and leads the way in creative problem solving. They have at least one partner that is a great marketer; someone who loves to be in contact with people and sell their firm to potential clients. These successful firms also have a partner or partners that oversee the day to day running of the business. They make sure that things run smoothly, that deadlines are met and that people have the information and tools necessary to do the work. Two of these three roles contain substantial business knowledge. Designers that have an interest in business would be well served if they would continue their education in a business program. The combination of business acumen and design experience can make a powerful combination.

# NOT MAKING MONEY IN ENVIRONMENTAL DESIGN

Most environmental design firms are for-profit organizations that are interested in creating substantial wealth for their owners, and providing a livelihood for their employees. Since the 1970's there has been a growing number of non-profit design firms established throughout the United States. These non-profit design firms exist to provide much needed design services for disadvantaged individuals and groups in a community. The poor, the disabled, the under-represented and other non-profit service organizations are among the groups that need good design help and receive it from these non-profit design firms. Non-profit design firms put together funding for their work from a wide variety of sources. They may receive funds from local government agencies to help fight blight in their cities, they might receive grants from charitable organizations or foundations, they may charge nominal fees for their services, or they may do fund raising within the community at large. The social connection between these firms and their communities is a powerful force that draws designers into these practices. The desire to serve the broader public is the motivation behind these design firms.

Being a non-profit firm does not mean that the employees don't get paid. They get paid, often at a competitive rate with for-profit firms in the area but the firm does not make a profit. Nobody is creating wealth within the firm or for the owner. What they are creating is incredible social wealth in the communities in which they work. This can be very satisfying environmental design work for those people that like to work directly with people in need.

# ENVIRONMENTAL DESIGN AND ECONOMICS

Economics is one of the systems of our society. It is a system to which environmental designers make a substantial contribution and it is a system that, to a great degree, controls environmental design.

**ECONOMICS:** 1; a social science concerned chiefly with description and analysis of the production, distribution, and consumption of goods and services    2; economic aspect or significance

Environmental designers are a part of the service sector of our economy, but they are also key players in the construction industry which is a major player in the economy. When the economy is healthy there is plenty of money for investment in new buildings, interiors, parks, and cities. When the economy is not healthy the environmental design fields suffer a great deal. Environmental designers feel a downturn in the economy very quickly. Design is one of the fields that are affected first since we prepare the conditions for construction. This reliance on the general economy and on the construction cycles is a pretty major drawback to the environmental design professions. In the last decade the economy has been good and the environmental design fields have flourished. We don't know what the future may bring.

The broadening base for environmental design in the 21st century has created a demand for environmental designers. This seems to have been happening in addition to the demand created by a healthy economy. The demand for environmental designers of all types has been very strong. Demand has been particularly strong for landscape architects and planners, and we don't see much change in that strong demand in the future. The graying of the baby boomers will also create a need for more environmental designers. Baby boomers are now the owners and partners in most of the environmental design fields around the world and they are approaching retirement age. This is already starting to create a bit of a leadership vacuum in the professions and opening up opportunities for younger environmental designers.

One of the great advantages of the environmental design field is that the skills and knowledge of environmental designers increases with age. The knowledge that you acquire will always be useful. Even though designers may retire, they don't have to and many practice their profession for their entire lives. They do this because they enjoy their work.

# Creativity and Collaboration

Throughout this book we have been presenting the environmental design fields as creative endeavors. We have said that designers are problem solvers that creatively combine many different ideas into coherent, meaningful, and moving physical spaces. But what does it mean to be creative?

**CREATE:** 1; to bring into existence  2b; to produce or bring about by a course of action  4a; to produce through imaginative skill  4b; to make or bring into existence something new[7]

Creativity, in environmental design, is a process in which the designer amasses a great deal of information, observation, analysis, experience, and insight and is open to the possibilities for unique combinations that might be applicable to the problem at hand. These unique possibilities lead designers to the creation of something new. Being creative is not something that you are just born with, nor is it something that can be adequately taught. Creativity is a combination of both innate talent and education. Probably the most important characteristic of creativity is the ability to be childlike. To retain the sense of wonder in things and to ask what some might think are inane questions are both important in making new and unheard of connections between previously unconnected elements. Connecting things in new ways is the essence of creativity.

Earlier in this book I introduced the nature of the work for each of the environmental design fields and provided some tools for design, such as the basic elements of design and the ways in which space are manipulated, combined and organized. I have included a design problem for you to ponder. Imagine that you are an architectural intern, working in an office and the boss walks up to you and asks you to work out a plan arrangement for a portion of a building he is working on. It is just about lunch time and he asks you to figure it out right after lunch. He gives you the following requirements:

- There are twelve major spaces that must be organized in an efficient manner into a cluster of some kind.

- Each of the twelve major spaces has two subsidiary spaces associated with it.

- All twelve major spaces must be accessed from a single entry point that is a part of the building the boss is working on.

It is a beautiful fall day and you decide to walk to lunch. On you way back to the office a leaf falls from one of the trees into your hand.

Now take out a piece of paper and figure out a simple plan arrangement using squares for the spaces.

What does the leaf have to do with this problem? On the surface, nothing. To a creative individual open to the possibilities of the world around them the leaf may offer insight into how this problem might be solved. See

[7]Mish, Frederick C. (1993). *Merriam-Webster's Collegiate Dictionary, Tenth Edition.* Merriam-Webster's, Inc., Springfield, MA.

Figure 5.24 . . .

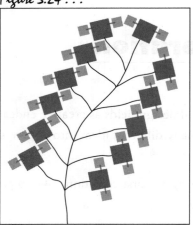

A possible plan solution related to an elm tree leaf. The grouping has one primary entrance, the major spaces each have two adjacent subsidiary spaces, and the major spaces are organized in a repetitive, linear fashion along the veins of the leaf.

Figure 5.25 . . .

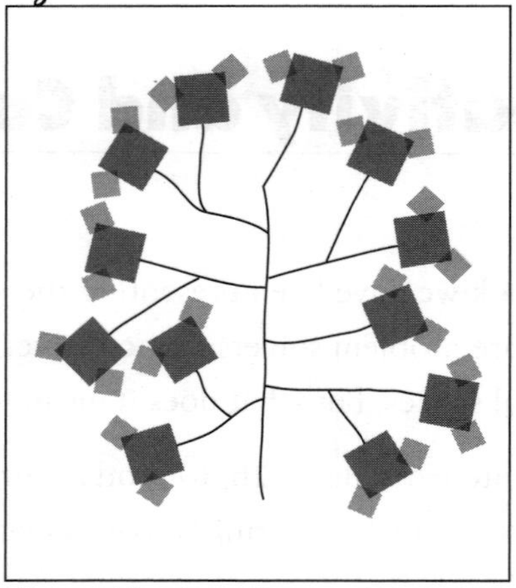

A possible plan solution related to an oak tree leaf. The grouping has one primary entrance, the major spaces each have interlocking subsidiary spaces, and the major spaces are organized in a repetitive, radial fashion along the veins of the leaf.

Figures 5.24 and 5.25 for two possible solutions to this problem. Each solution responds to a different type of leaf.

Until we know how this piece works with the rest of the building being designed, we really can't say which solution might be preferable. But, the designer was open to the requirements of the problem, as well as the possibilities of the environment to make connections and create something new.

A creative solution to an environmental design problem is hard work. It takes a great deal of information, observation, communication and analysis, as well as the development of multiple possibilities before the designer starts to close in on a best possible solution. It is so difficult to do because there is so much information and there is no single correct answer, just answers that are better.

The education of environmental designers is studio-based because the only way to effectively gain the knowledge and experience to make these difficult decisions is to practice the creative design process. Designers begin amassing experience in school and never stop learning. Each designer adds to his or her storehouse of knowledge and experience every time they do a different project. The knowledge that is acquired is so important to the success of design work. Designers develop an intuition about good design that must not be dismissed. Sometimes when looking at a design proposal, it is fairly easy to say that we don't like it, that it just isn't right yet. It is much more difficult to say why it isn't right yet. Designers just have to trust their intuition and try something else until it is right. In one scene of his movie *The Sketches of Frank Gehry*, Sydney Pollack, the producer/director, asks Frank Gehry why he is dissatisfied with a particular part of the project they are looking at. Frank Gehry, probably the most celebrated architect in the world today, responds that he just doesn't know, he only knows that it isn't right, and that they need to keep trying different approaches until it is right. Frank Gehry trusts his design intuition.

# COLLABORATION

Creativity and collaboration are linked together in this chapter for a very good reason. The two ideas are inseparable in today's environmental design fields. The importance of understanding the broader field of environmental design lies in the ultimate goal of creating the best environments for people and our planet. As stated many times before, the complexity of the problems facing environmental designers requires us to collaborate with each other. No individual environmental designer has the talent or ability that is in a strong team of designers. Designers bring their own creativity and experience to the process—to the betterment of all.

Not only do individual environmental designers bring the experience of their particular field to a collaborative team, they bring their own individual thinking styles and intelligence. I covered the importance of thinking styles earlier in the book, now it is time to talk about the importance of multiple intelligence. Up until a few years ago psychologists considered only one measure of intelligence—the intelligence quotient (IQ). Probably everyone reading this book has had an IQ test at some time in their life. A number of researchers working with intelligence, thinking and the acquisition of knowledge found the IQ measurements to be somewhat lacking. Their research showed that IQ tests and assessment tests such as the SAT and the ACT measured primarily the following:

- Literacy
- Memory
- Vocabulary
- General Comprehension
- Pattern Identification
- Spatial Ability
- Reasoning
- Math

Some of the things not being measured were:

- Perceptive Ability
- Verbal Communication Skills
- Teamwork
- Relationship Abilities
- Ingenuity
- Intuition
- Creativity
- Flexibility
- Mental Health

- Multicultural Awareness
- Varieties of Experience
- Ethical Codes

To the researchers, this presented serious problems when trying to describe the entire intelligence of a person. Howard Gardner proposed a series of multiple intelligences as an alternative to our traditional understanding of intelligence. His multiple intelligence list follows:

- Verbal/Linguistic Intelligence
- Logical/Mathematical Intelligence
- Visual/Spatial Intelligence
- Body/Kinesthetic Intelligence
- Musical/Rhythmic Intelligence
- Personal Intelligence
  - Interpersonal Intelligence
  - Intrapersonal Intelligence

Daniel Goleman has further explored the last item on this list, personal intelligence, in his work on and in his book titled *Emotional Intelligence*. This has been a much more satisfactory way to define intelligence. It is much more useful to us as environmental designers trying to put together effective teams to do our work. We all have intelligence in each of these categories but we have varying levels of intelligence in each one. For our teams to be truly effective and productive it is necessary for us to consider the individual talents and intelligences of each of the players. Who is it on the team that is particularly skilled in working with groups of people? Who is it that can write about the project in a way that is easily understood? Groups of people that think differently and are gifted in different ways help solve problems at a higher and better level.

Environmental design is an exciting field of endeavor for the future. The importance of the work that must be done, and the possibilities that individuals have to be involved with creative groups of people make environmental design a desirable field. Environmental designers can and will create substantial and important work that blends human needs with respect for the natural world.

# Selected Bibliography

Adjami, Morris, ed. (1991). *Aldo Rossi: Architecture 1981–1991*. New York: Princeton Architectural Press, Inc..

Antoniades, Anthony C. (1992). *Architecture and Allied Design*, 3rd Edition. Dubuque, IA: Kendall/Hunt Publishing Co.

Bartuska, Tom and Young, Gerald L. (1994). *The Built Environment: Inquiry into Design and Planning*. Menlo Park, CA: Crisp Publications.

Bender, Lawrence and David, Laurie, producers. (2006). *An Inconvenient Truth: A Global Warning*. Paramount Classics and Participant Productions, DVD.

Butler, Lawrence. (1997). *Clifford's Tower and the Castles of York*. Kate Jeffrey, ed. London: English Heritage.

Ching, Francis D. K. (1979). *Architecture: Form, Space & Order*. New York: Van Nostrand Reinhold.

Dal Co, Francesco. (1987). *Mario Botta: Architecture 1960–1985*. New York: Electra/Rizzoli.

Ehrlich, Paul R. (1968). *The Population Bomb*. New York: Ballantine Books.

Frank, Karen A. and Schneekloth, Lynda H. (1994). *Ordering Space: Types in Architecture and Design*. New York: Van Nostrand Reinhold.

Gardner, Howard. (1993). *Frames of Mind: The Theory of Multiple Intelligences*. New York: Basic Books.

Gardner, Howard. (1993, 2006). *Multiple Intelligences*. New York: Basic Books.

Goleman, Daniel. (1995). *Emotional Intelligence: Why It Can Matter More Than IQ*. New York: Bantam Books.

James, Jennifer. (1996). *Thinking in the Future Tense*. New York: Touchstone/Simon & Schuster.

Kostof, Spiro. (1995). *A History of Architecture: Settings and Rituals*. New York: Oxford University Press.

Lauer, David A. and Pentak, Stephen. (1995). *Design Basics*. Fort Worth: Harcourt Brace College Publishers.

Leadbetter, Ron. (1997). *Gaia*. Encyclopedia Mythica. www.pantheon.Org/articles/g/gaia.html accessed 18 February 2007.

Louis XIV. (1992). *The Way to Present the Gardens of Versailles*. Paris: Reunion des Musees Nationaux.

Lovelock, James. (1979, 1995). *Gaia: A New Look at Life on Earth*. Oxford: Oxford University Press.

Lupton, Ellen and J. Abbott Miller, eds. (1991). *the abc's of* ▲● ■: *the bauhaus and design theory*. New York: Princeton Architectural Press, Inc.

Macaulay, David. (1979). *Motel of the Mysteries*. Boston: Houghton Mifflin Company.

McDonough, William. (1992). *The Hannover Principles: Design for Sustainability*. Charlottesville, VA: William McDonough & Partners. Available at www.mcdonough.com/#.

McDonough, William and Braungart, Michael. (2002). *Cradle to Cradle: Remaking the Way We Make Things*. New York: North Point Press.

McHarg, Ian. (1967, 1992). *Design with Nature*. New York: John Wiley & Sons, Inc.

Meadows, Donella H. and Meadows, Dennis L., Randers, Jorgen, Behrens III, William W. (1972). *The Limits to Growth*. New York: Universe Books.

Mish, Frederick C. (1993). *Merriam-Webster's Collegiate Dictionary, Tenth Edition*. Springfield, MA: Merriam-Webster, Inc.

Moor, Malcolm and Rowland, Jon, eds. (2006). *Urban Design Futures*. Oxford: Routledge.

Osborne, Ken. (1995). *Stonehenge and Neighbouring Monuments*. London: English Heritage.

Rand, Ayn. (1943, 1971). *The Fountainhead*. New York: Signet-Penguin Books.

Rybczynski, Witold. (1999). *A Clearing in the Distance: Frederick Law Olmstead and America in the Nineteenth Century*. New York: Scribner.

UNFCCC. (2005). *Caring for Climate: A Guide to the Climate Change Convention and the Kyoto Protocol, revised 2005 edition*. Climate Change Secretariat, Bonn, Germany.

United Nations. (1998). *Kyoto Protocol to the United Nations Framework Convention on Climate Change*. United Nations, New York. Available at http://unfccc.int/2860.php

Wong, Wucius. (1972). *Principles of Two-Dimensional Design*. New York: Van Nostrand Reinhold.

Zelanski, Paul and Mary Pat Fisher. (1995). *Shaping Space*, 2nd ed. Fort Worth: Harcourt Brace College Publishers.